WILLIAMS-SONOMA

picnics and tailgates

Good Food for the Great Outdoors

Recipes by
Diane Rossen Worthington

Photography by
Chris Shorten

TIME
LIFE
BOOKS

TIME-LIFE BOOKS
Time-Life Books is a division of Time-Life Inc.
Time-Life is a trademark of Time Warner Inc. U.S.A.

Time-Life Custom Publishing
Vice President and Publisher: Terry Newell
Managing Editor: Donia Ann Steele
Director of New Product Development: Quentin McAndrew
Vice President of Sales and Marketing: Neil Levin
Director of Financial Operations: J. Brian Birky

WILLIAMS-SONOMA
Founder and Vice Chairman: Chuck Williams
Book Buyer: Victoria Kalish

WELDON OWEN INC.
President: John Owen
Vice President and Publisher: Wendely Harvey
Chief Operating Officer: Larry Partington
Associate Publisher: Lisa Atwood
Senior Editor: Hannah Rahill
Consulting Editor and Beverage Recipes: Norman Kolpas
Copy Editor: Judith Dunham
Design Concept: Patty Hill
Design: Kari Perin, Perin+Perin
Production Director: Stephanie Sherman
Production Manager: Jen Dalton
Editorial Assistant: Cecily Upton
Vice President International Sales: Stuart Laurence
Co-editions Director: Derek Barton
Food and Prop Stylist: Heidi Gintner
Assistant Food Stylist: Kim Konecny

In collaboration with Williams-Sonoma
3250 Van Ness Ave., San Francisco, CA 94109

A WELDON OWEN PRODUCTION
Copyright © 1998 Weldon Owen Inc.
814 Montgomery Street, San Francisco, CA 94133

Library of Congress
Cataloging-in-Publication Data

Worthington, Diane Rossen.
Picnics and tailgates : good food for the great outdoors /
   Diane Rossen Worthington.
     p.   cm. -- (Williams-Sonoma Outdoors)
   Includes index.
   ISBN 0-7835-4619-x (softcover)
     1. Picnicking. 2. Outdoor cookery. 3. Tailgate parties.
I. Time-Life Books. II. Title. III. Series.
TX823.W668   1998
641.5'78--dc21
                              97-28367
                                 CIP

First Published in 1998
10 9 8 7 6 5 4 3 2 1   12.18.18 SF

Manufactured by Toppan Printing Co., (H.K.) Ltd.
Printed in China

A NOTE ON WEIGHTS AND MEASURES
All recipes include customary U.S. and metric measurements.
Metric conversions are based on a standard developed for these
books and have been rounded off. Actual weights may vary.

A NOTE ON NUTRITIONAL ANALYSIS
Each recipe is analyzed for significant nutrients per serving. Not
included in the analysis are ingredients that are optional or added
to taste, or are suggested as an alternative or substitution either in
the recipe or in the recipe introduction. In recipes that yield a range
of servings, the analysis is for the middle of that range.

introduction

"Seating themselves on the greensward,
they eat while the corks fly and there is talk,
laughter and merriment, and perfect freedom,
for the universe is their drawing room and the
sun their lamp."

– JEAN-ANTHELME BRILLAT-SAVARIN

the environment

As you plan your outdoor meal, give careful thought to special opportunities provided by the setting. At a sandy beach you can build a fire pit, if regulations allow, for cooking or for keeping warm when evening falls. Whatever your destination, a large wicker hamper is one of the best ways to pack in food and supplies—and pack out any trash.

Freedom. That is the feeling you get when you enjoy a meal in the great outdoors. Your spirit instantly rises when you lift the lid of a picnic basket—or drop the tailgate of your automobile—to reveal the edible treasures you've prepared. Whether you're surrounded by hillside or meadow, woodlands or beach, or your own backyard, food tastes better when spiced with fresh air and sunshine.

A Reminder to Tread Lightly

Wherever you enjoy your meal, bear in mind that certain responsibilities accompany its pleasures. Travel on established roads and pathways so that you tread as lightly as possible on the landscape. Respect the rights of private property owners and take care not to pollute bodies of water. While observing wildlife, do not approach too closely or disturb habitats. Cleanup is easy when you bring trash bags to carry away disposables. Leaving the site in even better condition than you found it should be your goal.

setting the picnic

All of your senses—sight, sound, smell, and touch, as well as taste—keenly awaken when you partake of a meal in the outdoors. Be aware of them when selecting your location.

Picking the Best Spot

When you scout the setting to find the best place for your picnic, the view is often the most important element. Shifting your position even a few feet can make the difference between a mundane view and an awe-inspiring vista. Nature's music, be it melodious birdsong or lapping waves, helps set a mood of relaxation and well-being. A blossoming tree at a park, flowers filling a meadow, and the moist seaside air each add a distinctive, alluring scent to the occasion. Think about your physical comfort by picking the softest patch of grass or the smoothest sand. If convenience allows, bring cushions or lightweight folding chairs to make the seating even more comfortable.

When your meal is enjoyed beside a spring-fed stream or other refreshingly cool body of water, the sheltered banks or shallows serve as a natural beverage cooler. Torches or lanterns provide both illumination and romantic ambiance for an evening picnic. Citronella oil or candles can be lit to ward off bugs. To keep pests away from food, bring along wire or nylon-mesh fly walks. A supply of insect repellent will protect you and your guests.

equipment and packing

Sandwiches, classic picnic and tailgate fare, have an austere beauty when individually wrapped in waxed paper. Thermoses in an array of sizes and shapes keep hot dishes hot and cold dishes cold. Sealable storage containers stack neatly, protect food, and make serving easy. For cooking recipes on-site, bring along a small portable charcoal grill, briquettes, and utensils.

A well-stocked kitchen-supply store should carry all the equipment you need for packing your meal. Look for lightweight sealable containers and serving bowls, thermoses, and beverage dispensers. Standard wrapping supplies like waxed paper, plastic wrap, lock-top bags, and heavy-duty foil are indispensable. Invest, too, in artificial ice to keep beverages cold and perishables fresh. Ideally, dairy products, meats, eggs and mayonnaise should not be left out for more than two hours, or one hour in warm weather.

Before you pack your basket or hamper, line it with a towel to insulate it and absorb any spillage. Put heavier items and those in rigid containers on the bottom, then place more fragile items on top. You may also want to use an insulated cooler for transporting beverages.

For serving, bring plates, cutlery, utensils, glasses, and mugs, checking your supplies against those recommended for the recipes. Remember to include plenty of paper or cloth napkins, as well as kitchen towels and trash bags for cleanup.

beverages

limeade

1½ cups (12 fl oz/375 ml) lime juice
  (from 12–15 limes)
6–8 tablespoons (3–4 oz/90–125 g)
  superfine (castor) sugar
4½ cups (36 fl oz/1.1 l) cold water
18 fresh mint sprigs
ice cubes

✻ Put the lime juice in a large pitcher. Stir in 6 tablespoons sugar until it dissolves. Stir in the water. Crush the mint sprigs, then stir into the limeade. Taste and add the remaining 2 tablespoons sugar if desired. Cover and refrigerate until well chilled. Transfer the limeade, including the mint sprigs, to a chilled large thermos. Serve over ice cubes, tucking 2 or 3 mint sprigs among the cubes.

serves six | per serving: calories 81 (kilojoules 340), protein 0 g, carbohydrates 22 g, total fat 0 g, saturated fat 0 g, cholesterol 0 mg, sodium 1 mg, dietary fiber 0 g

watermelon-and-citrus agua fresca

6 lb (3 kg) watermelon, rind and seeds
  removed, cut into 1-inch (2.5-cm) chunks
1 cup (8 fl oz/250 ml) orange juice
½ cup (4 fl oz/125 ml) lime juice
¼ cup (2 fl oz/60 ml) lemon juice
1½ cups (12 fl oz/375 ml) cold water
1 tablespoon superfine (castor) sugar
ice cubes

✻ Working in batches if necessary, put the watermelon and citrus juices in a food processor and process until puréed. Place a fine-mesh sieve over

a large bowl and pour the purée into the sieve. Using a rubber spatula, press down on the fruit to force the juice into the bowl. Discard the pulp. Stir the water and sugar into the juice. Cover and refrigerate until well chilled. Transfer to a chilled large thermos. Serve over ice.

serves eight | per serving: calories 82 (kilojoules 344), protein 1 g, carbohydrates 19 g, total fat 1 g, saturated fat 0 g, cholesterol 0 mg, sodium 8 mg, dietary fiber 1 g

fresh raspberry spritzers

3 pt (24 oz/750 g) raspberries
1½ cups (10½ oz/330 g) superfine
  (castor) sugar
2 bottles (24 fl oz/750 ml each)
  sparkling wine or 6 cups (48 fl oz/
  1.5 l) sparkling water, well chilled
ice cubes
1 lemon, thinly sliced

✻ Put the raspberries and sugar in a food processor and process until puréed. Place a fine-mesh sieve over a small bowl and pour the purée into the sieve. Using a rubber spatula, press down on the fruit to force the juice into the bowl. Discard the seeds. Transfer the purée to an airtight container and keep chilled until ready to serve. To serve, place 3 tablespoons of the purée into each glass. Add ¾ cup (6 fl oz/ 180 ml) sparkling wine or water and ice. Garnish with a lemon slice.

serves eight | per serving: calories 309 (kilojoules 1,298), protein 1 g, carbohydrates 50 g, total fat 1 g, saturated fat 0 g, cholesterol 0 mg, sodium 10 mg, dietary fiber 4 g

mulled ginger cider with honey

8 cups (64 fl oz/2 l) apple cider
¼ cup (3 oz/90 g) honey
¼ lb (125 g) fresh ginger, peeled and
thinly sliced

❋ In a nonaluminum saucepan over low heat, combine the cider, honey, and ginger. Cover and warm, stirring occasionally, for 30 minutes. Transfer to a preheated large thermos. Include the ginger for a more pronounced ginger flavor. Pour into mugs to serve.

serves eight | per serving: calories 158 (kilojoules 664), protein 0 g, carbohydrates 40 g, total fat 0 g, saturated fat 0 g, cholesterol 0 mg, sodium 10 mg, dietary fiber 0 g

cinnamon hot chocolate

8 cups (64 fl oz/2 l) milk
½ lb (250 g) semisweet (plain) or
milk chocolate, broken into pieces
8 cinnamon sticks

❋ Put the milk, chocolate, and cinnamon sticks in a saucepan. Warm over medium-low heat, stirring frequently, until the milk is hot and the chocolate has melted completely. Transfer to a preheated large thermos. Include the cinnamon sticks for a more pronounced cinnamon flavor, or rinse off and dry the sticks and pack separately. To serve, pour the hot chocolate into mugs, placing a cinnamon stick in each mug.

serves eight | per serving: calories 285 (kilojoules 1,197), protein 9 g, carbohydrates 30 g, total fat 17 g, saturated fat 10 g, cholesterol 34 mg, sodium 123 mg, dietary fiber 0 g

spicy bloody marys

1 can (46 fl oz/1.4 l) good-quality
tomato juice
¾ cup (6 fl oz/180 ml) orange juice
3 tablespoons Worcestershire sauce
2 tablespoons prepared horseradish
2 tablespoons lemon juice
1 teaspoon hot-pepper sauce
such as Tabasco
1½ teaspoons celery salt
ice cubes
¾–1 cup (6–8 fl oz/180–250 ml) vodka
6–8 celery stalks, leaves attached

❋ In a large pitcher, stir together the tomato and orange juices, Worcestershire sauce, horseradish, lemon juice, hot-pepper sauce, and celery salt. Cover and refrigerate until well chilled. Transfer to a chilled large thermos. To serve, fill large glasses with ice. Pour 1 shot vodka over the ice in each glass. Add ¾–1 cup (6–8 fl oz/180–250 ml) of the tomato juice mixture. Use a celery stalk to stir each beverage, leaving it in the glass as a garnish.

serves six to eight | per serving: calories 126 (kilojoules 529), protein 2 g, carbohydrates 15 g, total fat 0 g, saturated fat 0 g, cholesterol 0 mg, sodium 990 mg, dietary fiber 2 g

appetizers and soups

grilled vegetable platter with picnic vinaigrette

Grilled seasonal vegetables make a colorful and festive beginning to a picnic. Grilled Marinated Flank Steak (page 81) and Picnic Potato Salad (page 59) would be good choices for the main course.

1 shallot, finely chopped

2 tablespoons red wine vinegar

1 tablespoon lemon juice

1 teaspoon Dijon mustard

6 tablespoons (3 fl oz/90 ml) olive oil

2 tablespoons chopped fresh flat-leaf
   (Italian) parsley

2 tablespoons chopped fresh basil

salt and ground pepper

2 red bell peppers (capsicums)

2 yellow bell peppers (capsicums)

4 Asian (slender) eggplants
   (aubergines)

4 zucchini (courgettes)

18 asparagus spears, trimmed and
   peeled if desired

6 plum (Roma) tomatoes, halved
   lengthwise

¼ cup (½ oz/15 g) assorted finely
   chopped fresh herbs such as flat-leaf
   (Italian) parsley and basil

✲ Prepare a fire in a grill. To make the vinaigrette, combine the shallot, vinegar, lemon juice, and mustard in a small bowl. Whisk in the olive oil, then add the parsley, basil, and salt and pepper to taste. Transfer to a container with a tight-fitting lid.

✲ When the coals are medium-hot, place the peppers on the grill rack and grill, turning, until the skins blacken and blister. Place in a brown paper bag, close tightly, and let stand for 10 minutes. Remove the peppers and peel off the charred skin. Remove the stems, seeds, and ribs. Cut into ½-inch (12-mm) slices. Place in a large storage container.

✲ Cut the eggplants and zucchini lengthwise into ¼-inch (6-mm) slices. Lightly coat with nonstick olive oil cooking spray and grill, turning once, until softened and lightly browned, 6–8 minutes total. Place in the storage container. Lightly coat the asparagus spears and tomato halves with cooking spray. Grill, turning once, until softened and lightly browned, about 5 minutes for the asparagus, 8 minutes for the tomatoes. Arrange attractively with the other vegetables in the container. Drizzle with the vinaigrette and sprinkle with the fresh herbs. Keep chilled until ready to serve.

serves six | per serving: calories 202 (kilojoules 848), protein 4 g, carbohydrates 17 g, total fat 15 g, saturated fat 2 g, cholesterol 0 mg, sodium 39 mg, dietary fiber 4 g

cucumber-avocado soup
with tomato salsa

A cool, creamy uncooked purée of cucumber and avocado
is accented by a spicy salsa. A purchased fresh tomato or tomatillo
salsa, available in the refrigerator cases of most food stores,
works well, or substitute a favorite recipe of your own. Serve with
Grilled Vegetable Sandwiches (page 72).

1 large ripe avocado, pitted, peeled,
  and cut into pieces
1 large English (hothouse)
  cucumber, cut into pieces
1½ cups (12 fl oz/375 ml) chicken
  broth

5 tablespoons fresh tomato or
  tomatillo salsa (see note)
3 tablespoons lemon juice
½ cup (4 oz/125 g) sour cream
¼ cup (¾ oz/20 g) finely sliced
  green (spring) onions
salt and ground pepper

✳ In a food processor, combine the avocado and cucumber and process
until smooth. Add the chicken broth, 3 tablespoons of the salsa, the lemon
juice, the sour cream, and the green onions and process until combined.
Season to taste with salt and pepper. Transfer to a bowl, cover, and chill for
at least 2 hours or for up to 8 hours.

✳ Transfer to a chilled thermos. Serve in small cups or bowls. Garnish each
portion with a dollop of the remaining 2 tablespoons salsa.

serves four to six | per serving: calories 156 (kilojoules 655), protein 3 g, carbohydrates 9 g, total
fat 13 g, saturated fat 4 g, cholesterol 10 mg, sodium 481 mg, dietary fiber 2 g

deviled eggs

The secret to perfect deviled eggs (photo page 28) is in the cooking: don't boil them and don't cook them too long, and you will avoid tough eggs with dreary gray circles around the yolks. For a variation, stir into the yolk mixture 1 teaspoon pesto and ¼ cup (1½ oz/45 g) bay shrimp, or ¼ cup (2 oz/60 g) chopped smoked salmon and 1 teaspoon lemon juice.

6 extra-large eggs, at room
  temperature
3 tablespoons mayonnaise
¼ teaspoon salt

pinch of dry mustard
ground white pepper
paprika
1 tablespoon finely chopped fresh
  chives

⁂ Place the eggs in a saucepan and cover with cold water. Place over medium-high heat and bring to a rolling boil. Immediately turn off the heat, cover, and let stand for 15 minutes. Transfer the eggs to a strainer and set under cold running water. Crack them all over and peel.

⁂ Cut the peeled eggs in half lengthwise. Scoop out the yolks into a small bowl. Mash the yolks with a fork and mix in the mayonnaise, salt, mustard, and pepper to taste until well blended.

⁂ Spoon the yolk mixture into the egg white halves and place in a single layer in a storage container. Dust with paprika and sprinkle evenly with the chives. Cover and refrigerate for at least 1 hour or for as long as overnight. Keep chilled until ready to serve.

serves six | per serving: calories 135 (kilojoules 567), protein 7 g, carbohydrates 1 g, total fat 11 g, saturated fat 3 g, cholesterol 249 mg, sodium 202 mg, dietary fiber 0 g

chilled zucchini-buttermilk soup

The key to the refreshing taste of this soup is first
chilling the soup base, then adding the fresh herbs and lemon juice.
Try serving the soup before Chopped Salad (page 42).

3 tablespoons olive oil

2 leeks, including ½ inch (12 mm) of
  tender green tops, finely chopped

6 zucchini (courgettes), about 1½ lb
  (750 g) total weight, thinly sliced

2 cloves garlic, minced

4 cups (32 fl oz/1 l) chicken broth

3 tablespoons finely chopped fresh
  basil

2 tablespoons finely chopped fresh
  chives

1 cup (8 fl oz/250 ml) buttermilk

1 tablespoon lemon juice

salt and ground pepper

✳ In a soup pot over medium heat, warm the oil. Add the leeks and sauté, stirring occasionally, until softened, 5–7 minutes. Add the zucchini and sauté until lightly browned, about 5 minutes longer. Add the garlic and cook, stirring, until softened, about 1 minute.

✳ Pour in the broth, cover, and simmer the soup until the zucchini is tender, about 15 minutes. Working in batches, transfer to a blender or food processor and process to purée. Pour into a bowl, cover, and refrigerate for at least 4 hours or for up to 8 hours. Remove from the refrigerator and add the basil, chives, buttermilk, and lemon juice. Season to taste with salt and pepper.

✳ Pour into a chilled thermos. Serve in small cups.

serves six | per serving: calories 138 (kilojoules 580), protein 5 g, carbohydrates 11 g, total fat 9 g, saturated fat 1 g, cholesterol 2 mg, sodium 721 mg, dietary fiber 1 g

salmon, cream cheese, and cucumber pinwheels

Serve these colorful and sophisticated pinwheels with Deviled Eggs (page 26). For the cream cheese spread, you can use the suggested herbs or substitute your favorites. The recipe can easily be multiplied to serve a crowd.

2 tablespoons cream cheese, at room temperature

2 teaspoons finely chopped fresh herbs such as chives, dill, burnet, and/or flat-leaf (Italian) parsley

1 flour tortilla, 10 inches (25 cm) in diameter

2 oz (60 g) thinly sliced smoked salmon

1 piece English (hothouse) cucumber, about 6 inches (15 cm) long

In a small bowl, combine the cream cheese and herbs and use a fork to blend well. Set the tortilla on a work surface and spread with the herbed cream cheese all the way to the edges. Cover evenly with the salmon slices.

Draw a vegetable peeler along the cucumber to create 6 thin slices about 6 inches (15 cm) long. Arrange the slices over the salmon.

Tightly roll up the tortilla, trim the ends, cover with plastic wrap, and refrigerate for at least 15 minutes, or for up to 4 hours, to let the ingredients set. Remove the plastic wrap and cut the roll into 8 pinwheel slices.

Transfer to a transportable container and keep chilled until ready to serve.

serves four | per serving: calories 92 (kilojoules 386), protein 5 g, carbohydrates 9 g, total fat 4 g, saturated fat 2 g, cholesterol 11 mg, sodium 199 mg, dietary fiber 1 g

vegetable-avocado salsa with baked tortilla chips

This colorful and spicy dip (photo at right) is ideal for a summer picnic.
If you prefer a milder flavor, use a jalapeño chile instead of the serrano.
You can also accompany it with blue corn tortilla chips.

for the salsa:

2 large tomatoes, peeled, seeded and
  diced

1 yellow bell pepper (capsicum),
  seeded and diced

1 large carrot, peeled and diced

1 cup (6 oz/185 g) peeled and diced
  jicama

½ cup (3 oz/90 g) corn kernels (cut
  from 1 ear of corn)

½ small serrano chile, seeded and
  finely chopped (see note)

2 tablespoons finely chopped fresh
  cilantro (fresh coriander)

2 tablespoons finely chopped fresh
  flat-leaf (Italian) parsley

2 tablespoons lime juice

salt and ground pepper

1 avocado, pitted, peeled, and diced

6 corn tortillas, 6 inches (15 cm)
  in diameter

salt and ground pepper

✳ To make the salsa, combine all the ingredients except the avocado in a
bowl. Cover and refrigerate for 1 hour.

✳ Meanwhile, make the chips: Preheat an oven to 400°F (200°C). Cut each
tortilla into 6 triangles by first cutting it in half, then cutting each half into
thirds. Working in batches, place the triangles on a baking sheet. Toast until
crisp, 8–10 minutes. Remove from the oven, place the triangles in a bowl,
season to taste with salt and pepper, and let cool. Repeat with the remaining
tortilla triangles.

✳ Remove the salsa from the refrigerator and spoon into a transportable
serving bowl with a lid. Keep chilled until ready to serve. Transfer the chips
to large lock-top plastic bags. Pack the avocado separately, and right before
serving add to the salsa and mix well to incorporate. Serve with the chips.

serves six to eight | per serving: calories 136 (kilojoules 571), protein 3 g, carbohydrates 22 g,
total fat 5 g, saturated fat 1 g, cholesterol 0 mg, sodium 52 mg, dietary fiber 5 g

cold curried eggplant soup

Aromatic curry powder adds an appealing bite to the delicate
eggplant. Serve chilled and follow with Greek Sandwiches (page 68).

2 tablespoons olive oil

1 yellow onion, chopped

2 teaspoons curry powder

1 large eggplant (aubergine), peeled
and cut into ½-inch (12-mm) cubes

4 cups (32 fl oz/1 l) chicken broth

1 lemon slice

½ cup (4 oz/125 g) low-fat plain
yogurt

1 tablespoon lemon juice

2 tablespoons finely chopped flat-leaf
(Italian) parsley

salt and ground white pepper

❧ In soup pot over medium heat, warm the oil. Add the onion and sauté,
stirring occasionally, until softened, about 5 minutes. Add the curry powder,
reduce the heat to low, and cook, stirring constantly, until the curry powder
is well blended and very aromatic, about 2 minutes longer.

❧ Add the eggplant, broth, and lemon slice, raise the heat to medium-high,
and bring to a boil. Reduce the heat to medium-low, cover, and simmer until
the eggplant is soft, about 35 minutes. Remove and discard the lemon slice.
Transfer to a blender or food processor and process to purée. Transfer to a
bowl and let cool to room temperature.

❧ Stir in the yogurt, lemon juice, parsley, and salt and pepper to taste.
Cover and chill for at least 4 hours or for up to 8 hours. Transfer to a chilled
thermos and serve in small cups.

serves four to six | per serving: calories 132 (kilojoules 554), protein 5 g, carbohydrates 13 g,
total fat 8 g, saturated fat 1 g, cholesterol 1 mg, sodium 823 mg, dietary fiber 3 g

eggplant dip with tomato relish and pita toasts

for the dip:

1 leek, including ½ inch (12 mm) of
   tender green top, finely chopped

3 cloves garlic, minced

2 tablespoons olive oil

2 tablespoons balsamic vinegar

salt and ground pepper

2 large eggplants (aubergines),
   peeled and coarsely chopped

¼ cup (⅓ oz/10 g) chopped fresh basil

1 teaspoon chopped fresh thyme

1 tablespoon capers, rinsed

for the relish:

2 plum (Roma) tomatoes, peeled,
   seeded, and finely diced

1 tablespoon olive oil

1 tablespoon balsamic vinegar

salt and ground pepper

for the pita toasts:

2 pita breads, plain or sesame

2 tablespoons olive oil

2 tablespoons grated Parmesan cheese

4–6 fresh basil leaves for garnish

❋ Preheat an oven to 400°F (200°C). To make the dip, lightly coat a large roasting pan with nonstick olive oil cooking spray. In the pan, combine the leek, garlic, oil, 1 tablespoon of the vinegar, and salt and pepper to taste. Add the chopped eggplant and toss to coat with the oil and vinegar. Roast, tossing every 15 minutes, until very soft, 1–1¼ hours.

❋ Meanwhile, prepare the relish: In a bowl, combine the tomatoes, oil, vinegar, and salt and pepper. Mix well. Taste and adjust the seasonings.

❋ Remove the eggplant mixture from the oven and let cool. Add the remaining 1 tablespoon vinegar and the basil, thyme, and capers. Mix well. Taste and adjust the seasonings.

❋ To make the pita toasts, preheat a broiler (griller). Split each pita in half, then cut each half into 8 triangles. Brush the top of each triangle with oil and then sprinkle with Parmesan cheese. Working in batches, spread the triangles on a baking sheet and toast in the broiler until brown and bubbly, about 3 minutes. Let cool. Repeat with the remaining pita triangles.

❋ Mound the eggplant dip into a transportable serving dish. Garnish with the tomato relish and basil leaves and keep chilled until ready to serve. Transfer the pita toasts to large lock-top plastic bags.

serves four to six | per serving: calories 277 (kilojoules 1,163), protein 6 g, carbohydrates 33 g, total fat 15 g, saturated fat 2 g, cholesterol 2 mg, sodium 258 mg, dietary fiber 4 g

pork brochettes with peanut sauce

The Indonesian satay, a skewer of delectable meat or chicken,
is the inspiration for these piquant brochettes. You can bring
the marinated skewers to a picnic or tailgate party, ready to be grilled
at the last minute, or grill them ahead and serve them chilled.
Either way, they are a great beginning to a party.

½ cup (4 fl oz/125 ml) orange juice

2 tablespoons lime juice

2 tablespoons vegetable oil

1 teaspoon chopped fresh oregano

1 teaspoon finely chopped fresh
 cilantro (fresh coriander)

½ teaspoon ground cumin

salt and ground pepper

1 lb (500 g) pork tenderloin, cut into
 1-inch (2.5-cm) pieces

for the sauce:

½ cup (4 oz/125 g) chunky peanut
 butter

¾ cup (6 fl oz/180 ml) coconut milk

1 tablespoon soy sauce

1 tablespoon honey

2 teaspoons peeled and minced
 fresh ginger

2 cloves garlic, minced

✳ In a bowl, combine the orange juice, lime juice, oil, oregano, cilantro,
cumin, and salt and pepper to taste. Whisk until blended. Thread the pork
onto wooden or metal skewers and arrange in a shallow nonaluminum dish.
(If using wooden skewers, first soak in water for at least 15 minutes.) Reserve
3 tablespoons of the marinade and pour the remainder over the skewered
pork. Cover and refrigerate for at least 6 hours or for up to 12 hours.

✳ Meanwhile make the sauce: In a bowl, whisk together all the ingredients.
Transfer to a small transportable container.

✳ Prepare a fire in a grill. When the coals are medium-hot, place the skewers on the grill rack and brush with the remaining 3 tablespoons marinade.
Grill until well browned, 5–7 minutes on each side. Remove from the grill
and arrange on a large plate or transfer to a transportable container. Serve
with the peanut sauce.

serves four to six | per serving: calories 401 (kilojoules 1,684), protein 25 g, carbohydrates 13 g,
total fat 29 g, saturated fat 11 g, cholesterol 57 mg, sodium 361 mg, dietary fiber 2 g

tomato-basil soup with parmesan cheese

This comforting soup tastes best with fresh ripe tomatoes. You can vary the flavor by substituting fresh dill for the basil. The soup can be made a day ahead and reheated just before pouring into a thermos.

¼ cup (2 fl oz/60 ml) olive oil

1 yellow onion, thinly sliced

1 carrot, peeled and finely chopped

1 celery stalk, finely chopped

1 clove garlic, minced

¼ cup (1½ oz/45 g) all-purpose (plain) flour

6 ripe tomatoes, about 3 lb (1.5 kg) total weight, seeded and coarsely chopped

¼ cup (2 oz/60 g) tomato paste

3 cups (24 fl oz/750 ml) chicken broth

¼ cup (⅓ oz/10 g) finely chopped fresh basil

1 teaspoon sugar

1 cup (8 fl oz/250 ml) milk

salt and ground white pepper

½ cup (¾ oz/20 g) cheese croutons

2 tablespoons grated Parmesan cheese

✻ In a soup pot over medium heat, heat the oil. Add the onion and cook, stirring occasionally, until translucent, about 3 minutes. Add the carrot and celery and cook, stirring occasionally, until the vegetables begin to soften, about 4 minutes. Add the garlic and cook, stirring, until slightly softened, about 1 minute longer.

✻ Sprinkle the flour over the vegetables, reduce the heat to low, and cook, stirring, until incorporated, 1–2 minutes. Add the tomatoes, broth, tomato paste, basil, and sugar, raise the heat to medium-high, and bring to a simmer. Reduce the heat to medium, partially cover, and cook, stirring occasionally, until the vegetables are tender and the flavors are well blended, about 20 minutes.

✻ Working in batches, transfer the soup to a blender or food processor and process to purée, making sure to leave a little texture. Return to the pan and place over medium heat until heated through, 1–2 minutes. Add the milk, stirring to combine, and season to taste with salt and pepper. Remove from the heat and pour into a heated thermos. Serve in small, heatproof cups, garnished with croutons and a sprinkling of Parmesan cheese.

serves four to six | per serving: calories 291 (kilojoules 1,222), protein 8 g, carbohydrates 31 g, total fat 16 g, saturated fat 3 g, cholesterol 8 mg, sodium 840 mg, dietary fiber 5 g

purée of vegetable soup with lemon and dill

Creamy potatoes, bright orange carrots, yellow summer squash, and green zucchini give this soup color, and dill imparts a fragrant garden freshness. The soup is also excellent chilled.

2 tablespoons olive oil

1 leek, including ½ inch (12 mm) of tender green top, finely chopped

3 White Rose potatoes, about 1 lb (500 g) total weight, peeled and thinly sliced

2 carrots, peeled and thinly sliced

2 crookneck squash, thinly sliced

2 zucchini (courgettes), thinly sliced

6 cups (48 fl oz/1.5 l) chicken broth

2 tablespoons chopped fresh dill

salt and ground white pepper

½ cup (4 fl oz/125 ml) half-and-half (half cream) or milk

1 tablespoon lemon juice

❧ In a soup pot over medium heat, heat the oil. Add the leek and sauté until softened, about 3 minutes. Add the potatoes, carrots, squash, and zucchini and sauté, stirring, until slightly softened, about 3 minutes. Add the broth and dill, reduce the heat to medium-low, and simmer, partially covered, until the vegetables are tender, about 15 minutes longer. Season with salt and pepper.

❧ Working in batches, transfer the soup to a blender or food processor and process to purée. Return the soup to the pot and whisk in the half-and-half or milk and the lemon juice. Taste and adjust the seasonings. Pour into a heated thermos and serve in small, heatproof cups.

serves four to six | per serving: calories 232 (kilojoules 974), protein 7 g, carbohydrates 27 g, total fat 11 g, saturated fat 2 g, cholesterol 9 mg, sodium 1,235 mg, dietary fiber 3 g

chilled artichoke halves with lemon vinaigrette

Artichoke halves make perfect containers for a delicious vinaigrette.
The artichokes can be made a day ahead and refrigerated until serving.

1 lemon plus 3 lemon slices

3 large artichokes

1 tablespoon olive oil

1 shallot, finely chopped

3 tablespoons lemon juice

1 tablespoon red wine vinegar

1 teaspoon Dijon mustard

1 tablespoon finely chopped fresh
  chives

1 tablespoon finely chopped fresh
  flat-leaf (Italian) parsley

½ cup (4 fl oz/125 ml) extra-virgin
  olive oil

salt and ground pepper

❊ Fill a large bowl three-fourths full with cold water. Halve the lemon and squeeze the juice into the water. Working with 1 artichoke at a time, cut the sharp points off the leaves with kitchen shears. Remove the small dry outer leaves from around the base. Trim the stem 1 inch (2.5 cm) from the base. Immediately place each trimmed artichoke into the lemon water.

❊ Soak all the artichokes in the water for at least 15 minutes to clean them. Drain and place upright in a large saucepan. Add water to a depth of about 4 inches (10 cm). Add the lemon slices and the 1 tablespoon olive oil. Cook over medium heat, partially covered, until the leaves pull off easily, 30–45 minutes. Remove from the pan and let cool.

❊ Meanwhile, in a small bowl, combine the shallot, lemon juice, vinegar, mustard, chives, and parsley. Whisk to combine and slowly whisk in the ½ cup (4 fl oz/125 ml) olive oil until incorporated. Season to taste with salt and pepper. Transfer to a container with a tight-fitting lid.

❊ Cut each artichoke in half. Using a teaspoon, scoop out the prickly choke and discard. Place the artichoke halves in a transportable container and keep chilled until ready to serve.

❊ Just before serving, spoon about 2 tablespoons of the vinaigrette over each artichoke half. Serve chilled or at room temperature.

serves six | per serving: calories 224 (kilojoules 941), protein 3 g, carbohydrates 10 g, total fat 21 g, saturated fat 3 g, cholesterol 0 mg, sodium 98 mg, dietary fiber 4 g

salads

chopped salad

Full of crunchy vegetables and chopped chicken, this salad can be served as a main course or as part of a salad buffet. For the vinaigrette, you can substitute ranch or blue cheese dressing.

2 skinless, boneless chicken breast
  halves, about 5 oz (155 g) each
1 head iceberg lettuce, cored and
  finely shredded
½ jicama, peeled and finely diced
½ cup (2½ oz/75 g) diced red bell
  pepper (capsicum)
½ cup (2½ oz/75 g) peeled, seeded,
  and finely diced cucumber
1 celery stalk, finely diced
1 carrot, peeled and finely diced

1 cup (6 oz/185 g) drained canned
  chickpeas (garbanzo beans),
  coarsely chopped
2 tablespoons red wine vinegar
1 tablespoon lemon juice
1 teaspoon Dijon mustard
1 shallot, finely chopped
6 tablespoons (3 fl oz/90 ml) extra-
  virgin olive oil
2 tablespoons finely chopped fresh
  flat-leaf (Italian) parsley
salt and ground pepper

✳ Place the chicken in a sauté pan and add water to cover. Place over medium-high heat and bring to a simmer. Reduce the heat to low and simmer, uncovered, until the chicken is no longer pink in the center when cut into with a knife, 10–12 minutes. Remove from the heat and set aside to cool in the liquid.

✳ In a large transportable bowl, combine the lettuce, jicama, bell pepper, cucumber, celery, carrot, and chickpeas. Toss well. Drain the chicken and finely chop. Add to the vegetables and toss to combine. Cover and keep chilled until ready to serve.

✳ In a small bowl, combine the vinegar, lemon juice, mustard, and shallot. Slowly whisk in the olive oil until incorporated. Add the parsley and season to taste with salt and pepper. Taste and adjust the seasonings. Transfer to a container with a tight-fitting lid.

✳ To serve, pour the dressing over the salad and toss to coat.

serves four to six | per serving: calories 314 (kilojoules 1,319), protein 19 g, carbohydrates 20 g, total fat 19 g, saturated fat 3 g, cholesterol 35 mg, sodium 158 mg, dietary fiber 7 g

coleslaw
with cider dressing

This sweet-and-sour cabbage salad makes an excellent companion for
any sandwich. It's also good with Grilled Marinated Flank Steak (page 81).
If you like caraway seeds, add ½ teaspoon for a slightly pungent accent.

4 cups (12 oz/375 g) shredded green
  cabbage

2 cups (6 oz/185 g) shredded red
  cabbage

1 carrot, peeled and shredded

¾ cup (6 fl oz/180 ml) mayonnaise

½ cup (4 oz/125 g) sour cream

1½ tablespoons sugar

3 tablespoons cider vinegar

2 tablespoons finely chopped fresh
  flat-leaf (Italian) parsley

2 cloves garlic, minced

salt and ground pepper

❉ In a large transportable bowl, combine the shredded cabbages and carrot.
In another bowl combine the remaining ingredients, including salt and pepper to taste. Whisk until smooth.

❉ Pour the dressing over the vegetables and toss well. Taste and adjust
the seasonings. Cover and refrigerate until the flavors are blended, at least
2 hours or for up to 8 hours. Keep chilled until ready to serve.

serves six | per serving: calories 279 (kilojoules 1,172), protein 2 g, carbohydrates 11 g, total fat
26 g, saturated fat 6 g, cholesterol 25 mg, sodium 185 mg, dietary fiber 2 g

summer celebration pasta salad

Light pasta salads are always appreciated on hot summer days.
To make a more substantial main-course salad, add 1 pound (500 g)
cooked shrimp (prawns), cubed or shredded chicken, or bay scallops.
For color, add julienned carrot and zucchini (courgette).

1 teaspoon salt

1 lb (500 g) fusilli or penne

1 tablespoon plus ⅓ cup (3 fl oz/
   80 ml) extra-virgin olive oil

2 lb (1 kg) ripe tomatoes, peeled,
   seeded, and coarsely chopped

5 cloves garlic, minced

½ cup (¾ oz/20 g) coarsely chopped
   fresh basil

¼ cup (⅓ oz/10 g) finely chopped
   fresh flat-leaf (Italian) parsley

3 tablespoons red wine vinegar

1 lb (500 g) fresh mozzarella cheese,
   cut into 1-inch (2.5-cm) cubes

½ cup (2 oz/60 g) grated Parmesan
   cheese

salt and ground pepper

❋ Bring a large pot two-thirds full of water to a boil over high heat and add the salt. Add the pasta, stir well, and cook until al dente (tender but firm to the bite), 7–10 minutes or according to the package directions. Drain, place in a transportable bowl, and mix in the 1 tablespoon olive oil to keep the pasta from sticking together.

❋ In a bowl, combine the tomatoes, garlic, basil, parsley, ⅓ cup (3 fl oz/ 80 ml) olive oil, vinegar, mozzarella and Parmesan cheeses, and salt and pepper to taste. Stir to mix well. Taste and adjust the seasonings.

❋ Pour the sauce over the pasta and mix well. Cover and keep chilled until ready to serve.

serves four to six | per serving: calories 838 (kilojoules 3,520), protein 34 g, carbohydrates 81 g, total fat 42 g, saturated fat 5 g, cholesterol 73 mg, sodium 608 mg, dietary fiber 5 g

asian noodle salad with salmon and snow peas

The coolness of citrus and mint enhances the flavor of the noodles and salmon. If Chinese egg noodles are unavailable, you can substitute linguine. The salad can be made a day ahead and refrigerated.

2 carrots, peeled and julienned

½ lb (250 g) snow peas (mangetouts), trimmed and julienned

¾ lb (375 g) salmon fillet

1 lb (500 g) Chinese egg noodles

1 tablespoon plus ¼ cup (2 fl oz/ 60 ml) canola oil

2 teaspoons Asian sesame oil

¼ cup (2 fl oz/60 ml) rice wine vinegar

1 tablespoon lime juice

1 tablespoon honey

2 cloves garlic, minced

1½ teaspoons peeled and grated fresh ginger

2 tablespoons finely chopped fresh basil, plus sprigs for garnish

2 tablespoons finely chopped fresh mint, plus sprigs for garnish

salt and cracked black pepper

Preheat an oven to 400°F (200°C). Bring a saucepan two-thirds full of water to a boil. Add the carrots and cook for 30 seconds. Using a slotted spoon, scoop out and immerse in a bowl of ice water to stop the cooking. Repeat with the snow peas, cooking them for 1 minute. Set aside.

Remove and discard any errant bones in the salmon. Place the salmon in a small roasting pan and bake until opaque throughout, about 12 minutes. Let cool, then shred into bite-sized pieces.

Bring a large pot of water to a boil. Add the noodles, stir, and cook until barely tender and still firm, about 7 minutes. Drain and rinse under cold running water until cooled. Drain well, place in a large transportable bowl, and toss with the 1 tablespoon canola oil to keep the noodles from sticking together.

In a small bowl, whisk together the ¼ cup (2 fl oz/60 ml) canola oil, sesame oil, vinegar, lime juice, honey, garlic, ginger, chopped basil and mint, and salt and pepper to taste. Pour the dressing over the noodles and toss to coat. Add the carrots and snow peas and toss again. Carefully toss in the salmon, keeping the pieces intact. Taste and adjust the seasonings. Garnish with mint and basil sprigs. Cover and keep chilled until ready to serve.

serves four to six | per serving: calories 617 (kilojoules 2,591), protein 27 g, carbohydrates 78 g, total fat 21 g, saturated fat 2 g, cholesterol 37 mg, sodium 49 mg, dietary fiber 4 g

roasted beets with orange vinaigrette

These beets are accented with an orange-flavored vinaigrette and toasted pecans. Walnuts may be substituted. If you want to serve a trio of salads, accompany with Green Bean and Sweet Pepper Salad (page 51) and Cracked Wheat and Vegetable Salad (page 50).

6 beets, about 2 lb (1 kg), trimmed
and scrubbed
¼ cup (1 oz/30 g) coarsely chopped
pecans
2 tablespoons orange juice

1 tablespoon balsamic vinegar
1 teaspoon Dijon mustard
¼ cup (2 fl oz/60 ml) olive oil
salt and ground pepper
1 tablespoon chopped fresh chives

❋ Preheat an oven to 425°F (220°C). Place the beets in a roasting pan and pour in water to a depth of ¼ inch (6 mm). Cover the pan with aluminum foil and roast the beets until fork-tender, about 45 minutes. Remove from the oven and let cool.

❋ Reduce the oven temperature to 350°F (180°C). Remove the skins from the beets and cut into ½-inch (12-mm) pieces. Transfer to a transportable bowl, cover, and refrigerate.

❋ Spread the nuts on a baking sheet and toast in the oven until lightly browned and fragrant, 5–7 minutes. Remove from the oven and set aside.

❋ In a small bowl, whisk together the orange juice, vinegar, and Dijon mustard. Slowly whisk in the olive oil until incorporated. Season to taste with salt and pepper and add the chives.

❋ Pour the dressing over the beets and toss to coat evenly. Sprinkle with the toasted nuts. Cover and keep cool until ready to serve. Serve chilled or at room temperature.

serves six | per serving: calories 161 (kilojoules 676), protein 2 g, carbohydrates 12 g, total fat 12 g, saturated fat 1 g, cholesterol 0 mg, sodium 97 mg, dietary fiber 1 g

cracked wheat and vegetable salad

If you want to substitute bulgur wheat for the cracked wheat, it will need to soak in the hot water for only 20–30 minutes. This salad (photo page 48) is good accompanied with grilled shrimp (prawns) or scallops.

1 cup (6 oz/185 g) cracked wheat

1¾ cups (14 fl oz/430 ml) boiling water

1 cup (5 oz/155 g) finely diced English (hothouse) cucumber

½ cup (2½ oz/75 g) finely diced red bell pepper (capsicum)

½ cup (2½ oz/75 g) finely diced, peeled carrot

1 tomato, seeded and finely diced

¾ cup (4 oz/125 g) crumbled feta cheese

¼ cup (⅓ oz/10 g) finely chopped fresh flat-leaf (Italian) parsley

2 tablespoons finely chopped green (spring) onion

2 tablespoons finely chopped fresh mint

6 tablespoons (3 fl oz/90 ml) extra-virgin olive oil

3 tablespoons lemon juice

1 teaspoon Dijon mustard

salt and ground pepper

✳ Place the cracked wheat in a bowl and pour in the boiling water. Let stand until the wheat has absorbed all of the water, about 1 hour. Drain the wheat in a colander, then place in a dry kitchen towel and wring out any remaining water. Transfer to a transportable bowl.

✳ Add the cucumber, bell pepper, and carrot to the cracked wheat. Mix with a fork so that the wheat stays fluffy and is not crushed. Add the tomato, feta, parsley, green onion, and mint. Toss gently to combine.

✳ In a small bowl, combine the oil, lemon juice, mustard, and salt and pepper to taste. Whisk to blend. Pour the dressing over the salad and mix again with the fork. Taste and adjust the seasonings. Cover and keep chilled until ready to serve.

serves four to six | per serving: calories 344 (kilojoules 1,445), protein 8 g, carbohydrates 32 g, total fat 22 g, saturated fat 6 g, cholesterol 20 mg, sodium 294 mg, dietary fiber 8 g

green bean and sweet pepper salad

A citrus-flavored dressing accentuates the sweetness of green beans and bell peppers (photo page 48). You can also add other vegetables, such as sliced carrots, mushrooms, or jicama. Serve alongside an Italian Hero Sandwich (page 66) or Roast Beef and Spicy Slaw Sandwiches (page 86).

1 lb (500 g) green beans, trimmed
1 yellow bell pepper (capsicum),
seeded and julienned
1 red bell pepper (capsicum), seeded
and julienned
¼ cup (2 fl oz/60 ml) lemon juice
1 teaspoon Dijon mustard

1 tablespoon finely chopped fresh
chives
1 tablespoon finely chopped fresh
flat-leaf (Italian) parsley
½ cup (4 fl oz/125 ml) extra-virgin
olive oil
salt and ground pepper

✻ Bring a saucepan two-thirds full of water to a boil. Add the beans and cook until tender-crisp, 7–10 minutes. Drain and immerse in a bowl of ice water to stop the cooking. Drain well and transfer to a transportable bowl. Add the bell peppers.

✻ In a small bowl, combine the lemon juice, mustard, chives, and parsley. Whisk in the oil until incorporated. Season to taste with salt and pepper.

✻ Pour the dressing over the vegetables and toss to combine. Taste and adjust the seasonings. Cover and keep chilled until ready to serve.

serves four to six | per serving: calories 229 (kilojoules 962), protein 2 g, carbohydrates 8 g, total fat 23 g, saturated fat 3 g, cholesterol 0 mg, sodium 32 mg, dietary fiber 2 g

salad niçoise

In this version of salade niçoise all of the ingredients are combined and mixed with a lemony dressing that can be prepared hours ahead. It is hearty enough to serve as a main course along with a loaf of crusty French bread.

1 lb (500 g) new potatoes, red-skinned, tan-skinned, or Yellow Finn

1 lb (500 g) green beans, trimmed and cut into 2-inch (5-cm) pieces

2 cans (12 oz/375 g each) white-meat tuna packed in water, drained and broken into chunks

1 small red bell pepper (capsicum), seeded and julienned

1 small red (Spanish) onion, thinly sliced and cut into ½-inch (5-cm) pieces

8 cherry tomatoes, quartered

½ cup (2½ oz/75 g) pitted Niçoise olives

2 tablespoons drained capers

6 tablespoons finely chopped fresh basil

salt and ground pepper

⅓ cup (3 fl oz/80 ml) lemon juice

1 teaspoon Dijon mustard

2 cloves garlic, minced

⅔ cup (5 fl oz/160 ml) extra-virgin olive oil

2 hard-boiled eggs, quartered

❄ Place the potatoes in a saucepan with water to cover. Bring to a boil, reduce the heat to medium, and cook, uncovered, until tender but slightly resistant when pierced, 20–30 minutes. Drain, let cool, and cut into bite-sized pieces. Place in a large bowl.

❄ Bring a saucepan three-fourths full of salted water to a boil. Immerse the green beans in the water and cook until tender but slightly resistant when pierced, 5–7 minutes. Drain and immerse in a bowl of ice water to stop the cooking. Drain well and add to the bowl with the potatoes. Add the tuna, bell pepper, red onion, tomatoes, olives, capers, 2 tablespoons of the basil, and pepper to taste and stir to combine.

❄ In a small bowl, combine the lemon juice, mustard, garlic, and 2 table-spoons of the basil. Whisk in the olive oil. Season to taste with salt and pepper.

❄ Combine enough dressing with the salad to moisten it. Toss gently. Arrange in a large, shallow transportable bowl. Place the egg quarters around the edges. Sprinkle the remaining 2 tablespoons basil on top. Cover and keep chilled until ready to serve. Serve any remaining dressing on the side.

serves six | per serving: calories 526 (kilojoules 2,209), protein 34 g, carbohydrates 24 g, total fat 34 g, saturated fat 5 g, cholesterol 115 mg, sodium 739 mg, dietary fiber 4 g

tropical fruit salad
with toasted coconut

This colorful fruit salad is excellent served alone or with a big dollop of your favorite yogurt spooned on each portion. Try flavors like piña colada, vanilla, or pineapple to jazz up the fruit.

½ cup (2 oz/60 g) shredded coconut

1 ripe pineapple, peeled, cored, and cut into ½-inch (12-mm) chunks

1 ripe papaya, peeled, seeded, and cut into ½-inch (12-mm) chunks

1 ripe cantaloupe, peeled, seeded, and cut into ½-inch (12-mm) chunks

1 ripe mango, peeled, pitted, and cut into ½-inch (12-mm) chunks

6 fresh mint leaves

※ Preheat an oven to 350°F (180°C). Spread the coconut on a baking pan and toast in the oven until golden, about 5 minutes. Set aside to cool.

※ In a large transportable bowl, combine all the fruit. Cover and keep chilled until ready to serve. Just before serving, sprinkle with the toasted coconut and spoon onto small plates. Garnish with the mint leaves.

serves six | per serving: calories 157 (kilojoules 659), protein 2 g, carbohydrates 33 g, total fat 4 g, saturated fat 3 g, cholesterol 0 mg, sodium 35 mg, dietary fiber 3 g

chinese shredded chicken salad

You can make this crunchy salad of cucumbers and carrots (photo at right) up to 4 hours ahead of serving. Begin with Cold Curried Eggplant Soup (page 31) and offer Plum-Almond Tart (page 100) for dessert.

4 skinless, boneless chicken breast
  halves, about 5 oz (155 g) each

¼ cup (2 fl oz/60 ml) soy sauce

¼ cup (2 fl oz/60 ml) unseasoned
  rice wine vinegar

1 clove garlic, minced

1 tablespoon peanut butter

pinch of sugar

pinch of Chinese hot mustard

¼ cup (2 fl oz/60 ml) Asian
  sesame oil

1 tablespoon chile oil

1 tablespoon canola oil

1 tablespoon sesame seeds

1 English (hothouse) cucumber,
  julienned

2 carrots, peeled and julienned

2 green (spring) onions, including
  tender green tops, thinly sliced on
  the diagonal

2 tablespoons finely chopped fresh
  cilantro (fresh coriander)

❄ Place the chicken in a sauté pan and add water to cover. Place over medium-high heat and bring to a simmer. Reduce the heat to low and simmer, uncovered, until the chicken is no longer pink in the center when cut into with a knife, 10–12 minutes. Remove from the heat and set aside to cool in the liquid.

❄ In a bowl, combine the soy sauce, vinegar, garlic, peanut butter, sugar, and mustard. Whisk to mix well. Slowly whisk in the oils until incorporated. Taste and adjust the seasonings.

❄ Place the sesame seeds in a frying pan over high heat. Toast, shaking the pan, until light brown, about 2 minutes. Immediately remove from the pan.

❄ Drain the chicken. Shred by tearing the meat into long, thin pieces. In a transportable bowl, combine the chicken, cucumber, carrots, green onions, and 1 tablespoon of the cilantro. Pour over the dressing and mix well. Taste and adjust the seasonings. Garnish with the sesame seeds and the remaining 1 tablespoon cilantro. Cover and keep chilled until ready to serve.

serves six to eight | per serving: calories 242 (kilojoules 1,016), protein 22 g, carbohydrates 6 g, total fat 15 g, saturated fat 2 g, cholesterol 50 mg, sodium 664 mg, dietary fiber 2 g

cherry tomato and corn salad

Vine-ripened cherry tomatoes and fragrant herbs complement the sweet fresh corn in this quintessential summer salad (photo page 58). It makes a good accompaniment to Grilled Marinated Flank Steak (page 81).

3 cups (18 oz/560 g) fresh white or
   yellow corn kernels (cut from about
   6 ears of cooked corn)
20 yellow or red cherry tomatoes,
   quartered
2 tablespoons finely chopped fresh
   basil

1 tablespoon finely chopped fresh
   flat-leaf (Italian) parsley
1 tablespoon extra-virgin olive oil
1 teaspoon red wine vinegar
salt and ground pepper

※ In a transportable bowl, combine the corn, tomatoes, basil, and parsley. Add the olive oil, vinegar, and salt and pepper to taste. Stir to combine. Taste and adjust the seasonings. Cover until ready to serve.

※ Serve at room temperature.

serves four to six | per serving. calories 121 (kilojoules 508), protein 4 g, carbohydrates 21 g, total fat 4 g, saturated fat 1 g, cholesterol 0 mg, sodium 19 mg, dietary fiber 4 g

picnic potato salad

The skins are left on the potatoes to give this salad extra color and texture. To spark up the flavor, you can add 2 tablespoons pickle relish or chopped red (Spanish) onion. This salad, along with Cherry Tomato and Corn Salad (page 57), pairs well with cold Lemon-Garlic Herbed Chicken (page 71) or your favorite sandwich.

3 lb (1.5 kg) new potatoes,
  red-skinned, tan-skinned, or
  Yellow Finn
¾ cup (6 oz/185 g) sour cream
¾ cup (6 fl oz/180 ml) mayonnaise
2 celery stalks, finely diced
2 tablespoons chopped green (spring)
  onion

2 teaspoons celery seeds
¼ cup (⅓ oz/10 g) chopped fresh
  flat-leaf (Italian) parsley, plus
  sprigs for garnish
2 hard-boiled eggs, coarsely chopped
1 teaspoon dry mustard
salt and ground white pepper

❋ Place the potatoes in a large pot with water to cover. Bring to a boil, reduce the heat to medium, and cook, uncovered, until tender but slightly resistant when pierced, about 30 minutes. Drain and let cool. Do not peel. Cut into 1½-inch (4-cm) pieces and place in a bowl.

❋ In a small bowl, combine the sour cream, mayonnaise, celery, green onion, celery seeds, chopped parsley, eggs, mustard, and salt and pepper to taste. Mix well.

❋ Pour the dressing over the potatoes and toss to coat. Taste and adjust the seasonings. Cover and refrigerate for at least 1 hour or for up to 8 hours.

❋ Transfer the salad to a transportable serving bowl and garnish with parsley sprigs. Cover and keep chilled until ready to serve.

serves six to eight | per serving: calories 407 (kilojoules 1,709), protein 7 g, carbohydrates 38 g, total fat 26 g, saturated fat 6 g, cholesterol 85 mg, sodium 191 mg, dietary fiber 4 g

asparagus with sun-dried tomato vinaigrette

Roasting the asparagus helps the spears retain their color and texture.
For the vinaigrette, use a good-quality Italian Parmesan cheese.
Dry Sonoma jack cheese can be substituted. To shave the cheese, draw
a sharp vegetable peeler across a block of cheese.

1½ lb (750 g) thin asparagus

¼ cup (2 fl oz/60 ml) water

1 tablespoon olive oil

¼ cup (1¼ oz/37 g) drained,
oil-packed sun-dried tomatoes,
thinly sliced

2 cloves garlic, coarsely chopped

2 tablespoons balsamic vinegar

2 teaspoons lemon juice

2 tablespoon finely chopped fresh
basil

½ cup (4 fl oz/125 ml) extra-virgin
olive oil

1 tablespoon grated Parmesan cheese

salt and ground pepper

shavings of Parmesan cheese for
garnish (see note)

✻ Preheat an oven to 400°F (200°C). Snap off any tough ends of the
asparagus stalks. Using a vegetable peeler, peel the outer skin from the
bottom 2 inches (5 cm) of each stalk. Place the asparagus in a roasting
pan. Add the water and 1 tablespoon oil. Roast until tender when pierced,
10–15 minutes. Drain, transfer to a transportable container, cover, and
refrigerate until well chilled, at least 3 hours or for up to 8 hours.

✻ In a food processor with the motor running, add the tomatoes and garlic and process until finely minced. Add the vinegar, lemon juice, and
basil and process to combine. With the motor still running, slowly add the
½ cup (4 fl oz/125 ml) oil and process until completely combined. Turn off
the motor, add the grated cheese, and pulse just to incorporate. Season to
taste with salt and pepper.

✻ Spoon about two-thirds of the dressing onto the chilled asparagus.
Reserve the remainder in a container with a tight-fitting lid to serve on the
side. Scatter the Parmesan shavings over the asparagus and keep cool
until ready to serve. Serve chilled or at room temperature.

serves four to six | per serving: calories 271 (kilojoules 1,138), protein 5 g, carbohydrates 7 g, total
fat 27 g, saturated fat 4 g, cholesterol 1 mg, sodium 65 mg, dietary fiber 2 g

spinach salad with pears, gorgonzola, and walnuts

Pears and toasted walnuts add a crunchy dimension to the pungent greens in this autumn tossed salad. Be sure to select a quality Gorgonzola that will crumble easily.

3 tablespoons sherry wine vinegar

1 tablespoon lemon juice

1 teaspoon honey-Dijon mustard

½ cup (4 fl oz/125 ml) olive oil

½ cup (2 oz/60 g) chopped walnuts

¾ lb (375 g) spinach, stems removed, torn into bite-sized pieces

2 heads Belgian endive (chicory/ witloof), cored and thinly sliced

1 firm but ripe pear, peeled, cored, and sliced

½ cup (2½ oz/75 g) crumbled Gorgonzola cheese

☀ Preheat an oven to 350°F (180°C).

☀ In a small bowl, whisk together the vinegar, lemon juice, and mustard. Slowly whisk in the olive oil until incorporated. Taste and adjust the seasonings. Transfer to a container with a tight-fitting lid.

☀ Spread the walnuts on a baking sheet and toast in the oven until lightly browned and fragrant, 7–10 minutes.

☀ In a transportable bowl, combine the spinach, endive, pear slices, and toasted walnuts. Sprinkle with the Gorgonzola.

☀ Cover and keep chilled until ready to serve. To serve, drizzle the vinaigrette over the salad and toss to mix well.

serves four to six | per serving: calories 350 (kilojoules 1,470), protein 6 g, carbohydrates 10 g, total fat 33 g, saturated fat 7 g, cholesterol 12 mg, sodium 261 mg, dietary fiber 3 g

main dishes

italian hero sandwich

This is the sandwich to make when you want an attention grabber! At a good Italian delicatessen, you'll be able to find the peppers and sliced meats, as well as a crusty loaf that will hold all the fixings.

¼ cup (2 fl oz/60 ml) red wine vinegar

1 teaspoon dried oregano

½ teaspoon dry mustard

salt and ground pepper

½ cup (4 fl oz/125 ml) extra-virgin olive oil

1 loaf Italian bread with sesame seeds, about 24 inches (60 cm) long, cut in half lengthwise

½ cup (2½ oz/75 g) seeded and chopped pepperoncini

½ cup (2½ oz/75 g) seeded and chopped cherry peppers

2 cups (6 oz/185 g) finely shredded iceberg lettuce

4 tomatoes, thinly sliced

5 oz (155 g) thinly sliced salami

5 oz (155 g) thinly sliced cappicola

5 oz (155 g) thinly sliced salami cotto

5 oz (155 g) thinly sliced mortadella

5 oz (155 g) thinly sliced provolone cheese

※ In a small bowl, combine the vinegar, oregano, mustard, and salt and pepper to taste. Stir to mix well. Whisk in the olive oil until incorporated.

※ On a work surface, lay out 3 long pieces of plastic wrap, placing them side by side and slightly overlapping. Place the bottom half of the loaf over the wrap. Spread the pepperoncini and cherry peppers over the bread. Scatter evenly with the lettuce and layer with the tomatoes. Drizzle with a few table-spoons of the dressing. Layer the meats, one at a time, over the tomatoes, making sure to distribute them evenly. Top with a layer of cheese.

※ Drizzle the remaining dressing over the cut side of the top of the loaf. Place on the layered sandwich and enclose in the plastic. Refrigerate for at least 1 hour or for up to 4 hours to develop the flavors.

※ To serve, unwrap the sandwich and slice into large pieces about 3–4 inches (7.5–10 cm) wide.

serves six to eight | per serving: calories 688 (kilojoules 2,890), protein 27 g, carbohydrates 41 g, total fat 47 g, saturated fat 15 g, cholesterol 73 mg, sodium 1,897 mg, dietary fiber 3 g

greek sandwiches

You can fill the pita pockets in advance or take the filling and pita breads to a picnic and assemble just before serving. Accompany these vegetarian sandwiches with Coleslaw with Cider Dressing (page 44).

2 tablespoons red wine vinegar
2 tablespoons lemon juice
2 tablespoons finely chopped fresh flat-leaf (Italian) parsley
1 teaspoon dried oregano
½ teaspoon dry mustard
salt and ground pepper
½ cup (4 fl oz/125 ml) extra-virgin olive oil
30 cherry tomatoes, quartered
1 English (hothouse) cucumber, coarsely chopped
½ small red (Spanish) onion, finely chopped
1½ cups (7½ oz/235 g) crumbled feta cheese
¾ cup (3½ oz/105 g) coarsely chopped, pitted Kalamata olives
6 sandwich-size pita breads

In a small bowl, combine the vinegar, lemon juice, parsley, oregano, mustard, and salt and pepper to taste. Slowly whisk in the olive oil until incorporated.

In a bowl, combine the tomatoes, cucumber, red onion, cheese, and olives. Pour over the dressing and toss to coat well. Taste and adjust the seasonings.

Carefully split each pita bread along the edge to open halfway. Using a large spoon, stuff the pita breads with the filling, dividing it evenly. Arrange in a transportable container, cover, and keep chilled until ready to serve.

serves six | per serving: calories 494 (kilojoules 2,075), protein 11 g, carbohydrates 43 g, total fat 32 g, saturated fat 9 g, cholesterol 32 mg, sodium 1,023 mg, dietary fiber 2 g

cold poached salmon with cucumber-avocado relish

A rich, crunchy relish is the perfect complement for poached salmon.
Serve with Asparagus with Sun-Dried Tomato Vinaigrette (page 60).

*1 English (hothouse) cucumber,
  seeded and finely diced*
*1 small, ripe avocado, pitted, peeled,
  and finely diced*
2 tablespoons chopped fresh dill
2 tablespoons olive oil

*2 tablespoons unseasoned rice wine
  vinegar*
1 tablespoon lemon juice
½ teaspoon sugar
salt
*2 lb (1 kg) salmon fillet, or 4 pieces
  salmon fillet, ½ lb (250 g) each*

❊ In a bowl, combine the cucumber, avocado, dill, oil, vinegar, lemon juice,
sugar, and salt to taste. Stir to mix well. Set aside.

❊ Remove and discard any errant bones in the salmon. Place in a sauté
pan and add water to cover. Place over medium heat and bring to a simmer.
Poach until the flesh is firm and flaky, 7–10 minutes, depending on the
thickness of the fillet or pieces; allow 10 minutes per 1 inch (2.5 cm) mea
sured at the thickest part. Remove from the heat and set aside to cool in the
liquid. When cool, drain and transfer to a transportable container. Cut into
4 pieces if using a whole fillet. Cover and refrigerate until well chilled,
about 4 hours.

❊ Spoon the relish over the salmon and keep chilled until ready to serve.

serves four | per serving: calories 454 (kilojoules 1,907), protein 46 g, carbohydrates 5 g, total fat
27 g, saturated fat 4 g, cholesterol 125 mg, sodium 108 mg, dietary fiber 1 g

lemon-garlic herbed chicken

This simple main-course chicken is also ideal for sandwiches, salads, and pastas. If you're cooking for a crowd, just increase the marinade by half and roast an additional chicken. The chicken can be prepared a day ahead and refrigerated until serving. To vary the marinade, you can substitute fresh tarragon and Dijon mustard for the rosemary and thyme.

¼ cup (2 fl oz/60 ml) olive oil

1 teaspoon finely chopped lemon zest

juice of 1 large lemon

1 teaspoon soy sauce

1 teaspoon finely chopped fresh
rosemary, plus sprigs for garnish

1 teaspoon finely chopped fresh
thyme, plus sprigs for garnish

3 cloves garlic, minced

1 shallot, finely chopped

⅛ teaspoon cayenne pepper

salt and ground pepper

1 frying chicken, about 3½ lb
(1.75 kg), quartered

1 cup (8 fl oz/250 ml) water

✳ In a large bowl, combine the olive oil, lemon zest and juice, soy sauce, chopped rosemary and thyme, garlic, shallot, cayenne, and salt and pepper to taste. Whisk until well blended. Taste and adjust the seasonings.

✳ Add the chicken quarters and turn to coat evenly. Cover and marinate in the refrigerator for 2–4 hours.

✳ Preheat an oven to 425°F (220°C). Remove the chicken from the marinade, reserving the marinade, and place on a rack in a large roasting pan. Pour the 1 cup (8 fl oz/250 ml) water into the pan. Roast, basting occasionally with the reserved marinade up until the last 10 mintues of cooking, until golden brown and the juices run clear when a thigh is pierced, 45–50 minutes. An instant-read thermometer inserted into the thickest part of a thigh away from the bone should register 180°F (82°C).

✳ Remove from the oven and transfer to a transportable serving platter. Garnish with the herb sprigs, then cover with aluminum foil until ready to serve. Serve warm, at room temperature, or chilled.

serves four | per serving: calories 516 (kilojoules 2,167), protein 48 g, carbohydrates 2 g, total fat 34 g, saturated fat 8 g, cholesterol 154 mg, sodium 208 mg, dietary fiber 0 g

grilled vegetable sandwiches

The key to making these luscious Mediterranean sandwiches is to grill the vegetables ahead and assemble them just before going on a picnic. Make sure to use a good-quality pesto from a well-stocked food store or delicatessen. For a large group, offer Grilled Chicken Sandwiches with Olive Mayonnaise (page 74) as well.

2 red bell peppers (capsicums)
1 large eggplant (aubergine), cut
  lengthwise into slices ½ inch
  (12 mm) thick
3 zucchini (courgettes), cut
  lengthwise into slices ½ inch
  (12 mm) thick

6 large sourdough or French rolls,
  cut in half
¾ cup (6 fl oz/180 ml) pesto
1 lb (500 g) fresh mozzarella cheese,
  cut into ½-inch (12-mm) slices
salt and ground pepper

❋ Prepare a fire in a grill. When the coals are medium-hot, place the peppers on the grill rack and grill, turning, until the skins blacken and blister. Remove from the grill, place in a brown paper bag, close tightly, and let stand for 10 minutes.

❋ Lightly coat the eggplant and zucchini with nonstick olive oil cooking spray. Grill, turning once, until the vegetables are soft and grill marks appear, 6–8 minutes total. Transfer to a platter.

❋ Remove the peppers from the bag, drain, and peel off the charred skin. Remove the stems, seeds, and ribs. Cut the peppers into ½-inch (12-mm) slices. Cut the eggplant and zucchini slices to fit on the rolls.

❋ Spread the bottom half of each roll with 1 tablespoon of the pesto. Top with the eggplant, then layer with the slices of zucchini, peppers, and cheese. Sprinkle with salt and pepper to taste. Spread the top half of each roll with another tablespoon of pesto, then place the top on each sandwich.

❋ Secure with toothpicks and cut in half, if desired. Transfer to a transportable container and keep chilled until ready to serve.

serves six | per serving: calories 654 (kilojoules 2,747), protein 26 g, carbohydrates 60 g, total fat 34 g, saturated fat 3 g, cholesterol 58 mg, sodium 798 mg, dietary fiber 5 g

grilled chicken sandwiches with olive mayonnaise

Enjoy this elegant version of a plain chicken sandwich (photo page 73) hot off the grill or cold. You'll find olive paste in a well-stocked food store or an Italian delicatessen. Serve with Picnic Potato Salad (page 58) or Coleslaw with Cider Dressing (page 44).

2 tablespoons lemon juice

1½ tablespoons Dijon mustard

6 skinless, boneless chicken breast
 halves, about 5 oz (155 g) each

¾ cup (6 fl oz/180 ml) mayonnaise

3 tablespoons olive paste

2 red bell peppers (capsicums)

6 seeded sourdough French rolls,
 cut in half

1 bunch arugula (rocket), stems
 removed

In a small bowl, combine the lemon juice and mustard. Arrange the chicken breasts in a nonaluminum dish and spoon over the marinade. Cover and refrigerate for at least 15 minutes or for up to 4 hours. In another small bowl, blend together the mayonnaise and olive paste, cover, and refrigerate.

Prepare a fire in a grill. When the coals are medium-hot, place the peppers on the grill rack and grill, turning, until the skins blacken and blister. Remove from the grill, place in a brown paper bag, close tightly, and let stand for 10 minutes.

Meanwhile, remove the chicken from the marinade, letting the excess drip off, and place on the grill rack. Grill, turning once, until no longer pink in the center when cut into with a knife, 10–14 minutes total. Remove from the grill and let cool for about 5 minutes.

Remove the peppers from the bag, drain, and peel off the charred skin. Remove the stems, seeds, and ribs. Cut into ½-inch (12-mm) slices.

Cut the chicken on the diagonal into thin slices. Spread about 1 tablespoon olive mayonnaise on the bottom of each roll. Top with the arugula and then the chicken slices, overlapping them slightly. Top with the bell pepper strips. Spread the top half of each roll with another tablespoon of olive mayonnaise, then place the top on each sandwich. Secure with toothpicks, cut in half if desired, and wrap in aluminum foil. Serve warm or chilled.

serves six | per serving: calories 673 (kilojoules 2,827), protein 50 g, carbohydrates 40 g, total fat 34 g, saturated fat 5 g, cholesterol 125 mg, sodium 1,162 mg, dietary fiber 3 g

potato-leek frittata

12 eggs

2 tablespoons finely chopped fresh
   flat-leaf (Italian) parsley

salt and ground pepper

1½ cups (6 oz/185 g) shredded sharp
   cheddar cheese

2 tablespoons olive oil

1 lb (500 g) red or white waxy
   potatoes, peeled and finely diced

1 leek, including about ½ inch
   (12 mm) of green, finely chopped

1½ teaspoons chopped fresh thyme

6 oil-packed sun-dried tomatoes,
   drained and sliced in half

✳ Preheat an oven to 350°F (180°C). In a bowl, combine the eggs, parsley, and salt and pepper to taste and whisk until well blended. Stir in 1¼ cups (5 oz/155 g) of the shredded cheese.

✳ Heat the oil in a 10-inch (25-cm) nonstick frying pan with an ovenproof handle over medium heat. Add the potatoes and leek and sauté, stirring frequently, until the potatoes are tender and the leek is golden brown, about 20 minutes. Stir in the thyme and season to taste with salt and pepper. Using a spatula, flatten the potato-leek mixture and pour in the egg mixture. Reduce the heat to medium-low and cook, stirring occasionally, until the bottom is slightly set, about 7 minutes. Arrange the sun-dried tomatoes around the perimeter of the pan. Sprinkle with the remaining ¼ cup (1 oz/30 g) cheese.

✳ Bake the frittata until puffed and brown, 10–15 minutes. Let cool. Slide onto a transportable serving platter and bring to room temperature. Cut into slices, then wrap the entire frittata in aluminum foil. Keep cool until ready to serve. Serve chilled or at room temperature.

serves six | per serving: calories 388 (kilojoules 1,630), protein 22 g, carbohydrates 19 g, total fat 25 g, saturated fat 10 g, cholesterol 455 mg, sodium 341 mg, dietary fiber 2 g

grilled bratwurst with onion marmalade

Serve this dish at a tailgate picnic in the autumn months when there is a chill in the air and you want something substantial and satisfying. If you prefer, use your favorite sausages. Accompany with a selection of mustards and some crusty bread. Serve Roasted Beets with Orange Vinaigrette (page 49) on the side.

¼ cup (2 fl oz/60 ml) olive oil

2 leeks, white parts only, finely chopped

1 large red (Spanish) onion, finely chopped

1 large yellow or Maui onion, finely chopped

¾ cup (6 fl oz/180 ml) dry red wine

¼ cup (2 fl oz/60 ml) balsamic vinegar

1 tablespoon sugar

1 teaspoon finely chopped fresh thyme

salt and ground white pepper

12 bratwurst, 2½–3 lb (1.25–1.5 kg) total weight, halved lengthwise

In a Dutch oven or other large nonaluminum pot, warm the oil over medium-high heat. Add the leeks and onions and sauté, stirring frequently, until well softened, 10–15 minutes. Add the wine, vinegar, and sugar, reduce the heat to low, and simmer, stirring occasionally, until almost all of the liquid has evaporated, about 10 minutes. The onions should be very tender and slightly caramelized. Stir in the thyme and salt and pepper to taste. Remove from the heat and let cool. Transfer to a transportable container. Keep chilled until ready to serve.

Prepare a fire in a grill. When the coals are medium-hot, place the bratwurst halves on the grill rack. Grill, turning as needed, until browned all over, 5–7 minutes total. Remove from the grill and divide among individual plates. Spoon some of the onion marmalade alongside and serve at once.

serves six | per serving: calories 797 (kilojoules 3,347), protein 31 g, carbohydrates 21 g, total fat 63 g, saturated fat 21 g, cholesterol 125 mg, sodium 1,176 mg, dietary fiber 2 g

portobello mushroom and goat cheese sandwiches

The meaty texture of portobello mushrooms combined with creamy goat cheese, sun-dried tomatoes, and fresh basil makes a substantial sandwich. Marinating the mushrooms before grilling prevents them from drying out. The sandwiches can be served warm or chilled.

1 cup (8 fl oz/250 ml) plus
  2 tablespoons olive oil
6 tablespoons (3 fl oz/90 ml)
  balsamic vinegar
3 cloves garlic, minced
2 shallots, minced
salt and ground pepper

6 portobello mushrooms, about 1½ lb
  (750 g), brushed clean and stems
  removed
6 round sourdough rolls, cut in half
1½ cups (7½ oz/235 g) crumbled goat
  cheese
12 oil-packed sun-dried tomatoes,
  drained and sliced in half
24 fresh basil leaves

❃ In a small bowl, whisk together the oil, vinegar, garlic, shallots, and salt and pepper to taste. Arrange the mushroom caps in a single layer in a shallow, nonaluminum dish. Pour half of the marinade over the mushrooms and reserve the remainder. Cover and marinate at room temperature for 1 hour, turning after 30 minutes.

❃ Prepare a fire in a grill. Lightly oil the grill rack. When the coals are hot, remove the mushrooms from the marinade, place on the grill rack, and weight with a large frying pan. Grill the mushrooms until tender and seared on each side, about 4 minutes total.

❃ Drizzle about 1 tablespoon of the reserved marinade on each roll half. Place a mushroom on the bottom half of each roll. Sprinkle the top half with goat cheese, then cover with sun-dried tomatoes and basil leaves. Place the halves together. Secure each sandwich with toothpicks, cut in half, and wrap in aluminum foil. Keep chilled until ready to serve.

serves six | per serving: calories 606 (kilojoules 2,545), protein 17 g, carbohydrates 44 g, total fat 42 g, saturated fat 11 g, cholesterol 28 mg, sodium 653 mg, dietary fiber 5 g

bake-ahead barbecued chicken

Marinating and roasting chicken before grilling it makes the meat flavorful and juicy. You can roast the chicken in the morning, refrigerate it, and then grill the pieces just before serving. Use your favorite purchased barbecue sauce for finishing the chicken on the grill.

½ cup (4 fl oz/125 ml) orange juice
1 shallot, finely chopped
2 teaspoons honey Dijon mustard
salt and ground pepper

2 frying chickens, about 3½ lb
(1.75 kg) each, cut into pieces
¾ cup (6 fl oz/180 ml) barbecue
sauce

❈ In a small bowl, combine the orange juice, shallot, mustard, and salt and pepper to taste. Arrange the chicken pieces in a large, shallow, non-aluminum dish and pour the marinade evenly over the chicken to coat it well. Cover and marinate in the refrigerator for 2–4 hours.

❈ Preheat an oven to 375°F (190°C). Remove the chicken from the marinade and place in a roasting pan large enough to hold the pieces comfortably in a single layer. Pour the marinade over the chicken. Cover the pan tightly with aluminum foil. Roast until the juices run clear when the chicken is pierced, about 35 minutes. The chicken should be just barely done. Remove from the oven and transfer to a platter. Pour the juices into a bowl, add the barbecue sauce, and stir to combine. Keep chilled until ready to grill.

❈ Prepare a fire in a grill. When the coals are medium-hot, place the chicken pieces on the rack and grill, turning once and basting occasionally with the sauce, until the skin is very crisp and brown, 10–15 minutes total. Remove from the grill and serve at once with the remaining sauce alongside.

serves six to eight | per serving: calories 510 (kilojoules 2,142), protein 55 g, carbohydrates 6 g, total fat 28 g, saturated fat 8 g, cholesterol 176 mg, sodium 383 mg, dietary fiber 0 g

grilled marinated flank steak

This steak is ideal for a picnic. The slices can be layered with tomatoes and watercress on French rolls spread with a chili-flavored mayonnaise. Serve with Green Bean and Sweet Pepper Salad (page 51).

2 tablespoons olive oil

2 tablespoons chili sauce

1 tablespoon soy sauce

1 teaspoon grated orange zest

1 teaspoon grated lemon zest

2 tablespoons orange juice

1 tablespoon lemon juice

2 cloves garlic, minced

1 teaspoon peeled and minced fresh ginger

¼ teaspoon ground pepper

2 lb (1 kg) flank steak

✳ In a small bowl, combine the oil, chili sauce, soy sauce, orange and lemon zest and juice, garlic, ginger, and pepper. Whisk until well blended. Taste and adjust the seasonings. Place the flank steak flat in large, shallow, nonaluminum dish. Pour the marinade over the steak. Cover and marinate in the refrigerator for 2–4 hours.

✳ Prepare a fire in a grill. When the coals are medium-hot, remove the steak from the marinade, letting the excess drip off. Discard the marinade. Grill until grill marks appear, 5–7 minutes on each side for medium-rare. Transfer to a carving board and thinly slice across the grain. Let cool, place in a storage container, and pour the juices from the carving board over the meat. Chill for at least 4 hours or as long as overnight.

serves four to six | per serving: calories 331 (kilojoules 1,390), protein 35 g, carbohydrates 2 g, total fat 19 g, saturated fat 7 g, cholesterol 90 mg, sodium 256 mg, dietary fiber 0 g

perfect grilled hamburgers

The best-quality meat is mixed with icy water and sweet tomato-chili sauce to create a juicy burger embellished with a dollop of olive paste. The burgers should be served right after grilling, so make sure to transport the meat in a cooler and take along a spatula.

2 lb (1 kg) ground sirloin

¼ cup (2 fl oz/60 ml) ice water

¼ cup (2 fl oz/60 ml) chili sauce

6 onion rolls, cut in half

6 tablespoons (3 oz/90 g) olive paste

6 iceberg or red romaine (cos) lettuce leaves

6 thick tomato slices

Dijon mustard to taste

pickle relish to taste

※ In a bowl, thoroughly mix the ground sirloin with the ice water and chili sauce. Shape into 6 thick patties. Cover and refrigerate until ready to grill.

※ Prepare a fire in a grill. When the coals are medium-hot, place the onion rolls on the grill rack, cut sides down, and toast until lightly browned, about 2 minutes. Transfer to a platter.

※ Place the patties on the grill rack and grill until grill marks appear on the first side, 3–4 minutes. Turn and grill on the second side, 4–6 minutes longer for medium-rare. Remove from the grill and set on the bottoms of the rolls. Top each burger with 1 tablespoon olive paste, a lettuce leaf, and a tomato slice, then with the top half of the roll. Serve immediately with the mustard and relish on the side.

serves six | per serving: calories 533 (kilojoules 2,239), protein 34 g, carbohydrates 35 g, total fat 28 g, saturated fat 9 g, cholesterol 95 mg, sodium 1,059 mg, dietary fiber 1 g

ratatouille tart

1 cup (5 oz/155 g) all-purpose
  (plain) flour

pinch of salt

6 tablespoons (3 oz/90 g) frozen
  unsalted butter, cut into pieces

¼ cup (2 fl oz/60 ml) ice water

1 small eggplant (aubergine), about
  1¼ lb (625 g), peeled and finely diced

6 tablespoons (3 fl oz/90 ml) olive oil

2 shallots, finely chopped

½ lb (250 g) white mushrooms, sliced

1 small red bell pepper (capsicum),
  seeded and diced

2 cloves garlic, minced

salt and ground pepper

3 eggs, beaten

1 cup (8 oz/250 ml) crushed tomatoes

2 tablespoons finely chopped fresh
  flat-leaf (Italian) parsley

¼ cup (⅓ oz/10 g) chopped fresh basil

1 teaspoon chopped fresh thyme

5 tablespoons grated Parmesan
  cheese

3 tablespoons Dijon mustard

5 tablespoons shredded Gruyère cheese

6 cherry tomatoes, halved

❋ Preheat an oven to 375°F (190°C). In a food processor, combine the flour
and salt and process to blend. Add the butter and process until the mixture
resembles coarse meal, 5–10 seconds. With the motor running, add the
water until the dough just comes together. On a floured work surface, press
the dough into a disk. Roll out to fit an 11-inch (28-cm) tart pan with a
removable bottom. Trim even with the rim. Place on a baking sheet. Prick
the bottom and sides with a fork, line with waxed paper, and fill with pie
weights. Bake for 20–25 minutes. Let cool. Remove the paper and weights.

❋ Place the eggplant in a colander, sprinkle with salt, and let stand for 15
minutes. Rinse and pat dry. In a frying pan over medium heat, heat the oil.
Add the shallots and sauté until soft, 3 minutes. Add the eggplant, mushrooms, and red pepper and sauté, stirring, until soft, 7–10 minutes. Add the
garlic and cook for 1 minute. Season with salt and pepper. Transfer to a bowl.

❋ In small bowl, stir together the eggs, crushed tomatoes, herbs, 2 tablespoons of the Parmesan cheese, and the eggplant mixture to make the filling. Spread the mustard over the baked pastry shell. Sprinkle with the
Gruyère. Return to the oven and bake until the cheese just begins to melt,
5–7 minutes. Pour in the filling. Arrange the cherry tomatoes around the
outside of the tart. Sprinkle the remaining 3 tablespoons Parmesan cheese
over the top. Bake until just set, 25–30 minutes. Let cool, then remove the
sides and transfer to a plate. Serve warm or at room temperature.

serves six | per serving: calories 440 (kilojoules 1,848), protein 11 g, carbohydrates 30 g, total fat
31 g, saturated fat 11 g, cholesterol 146 mg, sodium 359 mg, dietary fiber 3 g

roast beef and spicy slaw sandwiches

These sandwiches are quick and easy to prepare when you use a good-quality roast beef from a local delicatessen. Take along a platter of raw vegetables and serve Oatmeal Chocolate-Chunk Cookies (page 95) for dessert.

½ cup (4 fl oz/125 ml) plus
  6 teaspoons mayonnaise
2 tablespoons lemon juice
1 tablespoon plus 1 teaspoon
  prepared horseradish
1 garlic clove, minced

1 teaspoon caraway seeds
salt and ground pepper
3 cups (9 oz/280 g) finely shredded
  green cabbage
6 onion rolls, cut in half
1½ lb (750 g) thinly sliced rare roast
  beef

⚜ In a bowl, combine the ½ cup (4 fl oz/125 ml) mayonnaise, the lemon juice, horseradish, garlic, caraway seeds, and salt and pepper to taste. Mix to combine. Add the cabbage and toss to coat.

⚜ Spread the bottom half of each roll with 1 teaspoon of the remaining mayonnaise. Top with slices of the roast beef and then with the slaw. Place the top on each sandwich and secure with toothpicks. Cut in half, if desired. Wrap in aluminum foil and keep chilled until ready to serve.

serves six | per serving: calories 487 (kilojoules 2,045), protein 28 g, carbohydrates 35 g, total fat 27 g, saturated fat 5 g, cholesterol 64 mg, sodium 1,594 mg, dietary fiber 2 g

lavash wrap with hummus and honey-roasted turkey

For these Middle Eastern–influenced pinwheel sandwiches, seek out lavash, hummus, and honey-roasted turkey breast meat from a well-stocked food store or delicatessen. Allow three pinwheel slices per person, depending on how many other dishes you are serving.

1 lavash piece, about 14 by 22 inches
  (35 by 55 cm)
¾ cup (6 oz/185 g) hummus

¼ lb (125 g) thinly sliced,
  honey-roasted turkey breast
4–6 large spinach leaves, stems
  removed

🌟 Place the lavash on a work surface. Cover with a thin layer of hummus, spreading it all the way to the edges. Cover evenly with the turkey slices. Place the spinach leaves lengthwise down the center.

🌟 Starting with a long side, tightly roll the lavash and filling so they are compact. Trim the ends. Enclose in plastic wrap and refrigerate until set, about 30 minutes.

🌟 Cut the lavash roll into slices 1½ inches (4 cm) thick. Arrange in a large transportable container, cover, and keep chilled until ready to serve.

serves four | per serving: calories 224 (kilojoules 941), protein 14 g, carbohydrates 32 g, total fat 5 g, saturated fat 0 g, cholesterol 12 mg, sodium 578 mg, dietary fiber 3 g

desserts

open-faced apple-pear tart

This no-fail tart is easy to make. You prepare the pastry, place the fruit on it, and then just pull up the edges of the crust for a rustic presentation.

for the pastry:

1¼ cups (6½ oz/220 g) all-purpose
  (plain) flour

1 teaspoon sugar

¼ teaspoon salt

½ cup (4 oz/125 g) frozen unsalted
  butter, cut into small pieces

2 tablespoons ice water, or
  as needed

for the filling:

5 tablespoons sugar

2 tablespoons all-purpose (plain)
  flour

3 medium or 2 large Granny Smith
  or Golden Delicious apples, peeled
  and cut into ½-inch (12-mm) pieces

3 medium or 2 large firm but ripe
  Bosc or Anjou pears, peeled and cut
  into ½-inch (12-mm) pieces

❧ To make the dough, place the flour, sugar, and salt in a food processor. Process for about 5 seconds to blend. Add the butter and the ice water and process until the mixture has a crumblike texture and just begins to form a ball, 5–10 seconds, adding more ice water if the mixture is too dry. On a lightly floured surface, press the dough into a disk. Place a 10-inch (25-cm) springform or tart pan on a heavy rimmed baking sheet. Roll out the dough into a 13-inch (33-cm) round. Drape over the rolling pin and transfer to the pan, allowing the 3-inch (7.5-cm) overhang to lay flat on the baking sheet. Refrigerate while making the filling.

❧ Preheat an oven to 400°F (200°C). To make the filling, in a bowl, combine 1 tablespoon each of the sugar and flour, the apples, and the pears. Sprinkle 2 more tablespoons of the sugar and the remaining 1 tablespoon flour evenly over the tart pastry. Arrange the fruit mixture in the center and fold the dough edges up to create a free-form tart with the fruit visible in the center. Brush the dough with water and sprinkle the remaining 2 tablespoons sugar over the fruit.

❧ Bake until the filling is bubbling and the crust is caramelized, 40–45 minutes. Let cool at least 20 minutes on a rack. Slide the tart pan onto a transportable basket. Serve at room temperature.

serves six | per serving: calories 390 (kilojoules 1,638), protein 4 g, carbohydrates 60 g, total fat 16 g, saturated fat 10 g, cholesterol 41 mg, sodium 93 mg, dietary fiber 4 g

gingerbread cake

This cake holds up well, and making it a day ahead actually improves the flavor. If you like, garnish each serving with whipped cream.

2 cups (10 oz/315 g) all-purpose (plain) flour

1 tablespoon ground ginger

2 teaspoons unsweetened cocoa powder

2 teaspoons ground cinnamon

½ teaspoon baking soda (bicarbonate of soda)

½ teaspoon salt

½ cup (4 oz/125 g) unsalted butter

½ cup (3½ oz/105 g) firmly packed dark brown sugar

½ cup (5½ oz/170 g) dark molasses

2 eggs

3 tablespoons finely chopped crystallized ginger

1 cup (8 fl oz/250 ml) buttermilk

¼ cup (2 oz/60 g) sour cream

❧ Preheat an oven to 350°F (180°C). Butter a 9-inch (23-cm) square baking pan. In a bowl, combine the flour, ground ginger, cocoa powder, cinnamon, baking soda, and salt. Stir to distribute the spices.

❧ In another bowl, cream the butter using an electric mixer. Add the sugar and beat until creamy, about 3 minutes. Beat in the molasses, eggs, and crystallized ginger. Mix until combined. Beat in half of the flour mixture alternately with the buttermilk and sour cream. Beat in the remaining flour mixture. Pour into the prepared pan and bake until a wooden skewer inserted into the center comes out clean, 40–45 minutes. Transfer to a rack and let cool. Cut the cake into squares. Place in a transportable container. Serve at room temperature.

serves six to eight | per serving: calories 455 (kilojoules 1,911), protein 8 g, carbohydrates 68 g, total fat 18 g, saturated fat 10 g, cholesterol 103 mg, sodium 330 mg, dietary fiber 1 g

blackberry-nectarine buckle

A buckle is an old-fashioned dessert that makes a fine finish to any picnic.
Try it with Cold Poached Salmon with Cucumber-Avocado Relish
(page 69) and Cherry Tomato and Corn Salad (page 57).

½ cup (2 oz/60 g) coarsely chopped
  pecans

2½ cups (12½ oz/390 g) all-purpose
  (plain) flour

½ cup (3½ oz/105 g) firmly packed
  dark brown sugar

1 cup (8 oz/250 g) granulated sugar

½ teaspoon ground cinnamon

pinch of ground nutmeg

pinch of ground ginger

1 cup (8 oz/250 g) unsalted butter

1 egg

2 teaspoons baking powder

½ teaspoon ground ginger

½ cup (4 fl oz/125 ml) milk

1 pt (8 oz/250 g) blackberries

3 nectarines, peeled, pitted, and cut
  into ¼-inch (6-mm) pieces

❈ Preheat an oven to 350°F (180°C). Butter and flour a 9-by-13-inch (23-by-33-cm) baking dish. Spread the pecans on a baking sheet and toast in the oven until lightly browned, 5–7 minutes. Let cool.

❈ In a bowl, combine the pecans, ½ cup (2½ oz/75 g) of the flour, the brown sugar, ¼ cup (2 oz/60 g) of the granulated sugar, the cinnamon, the nutmeg, and the ginger. Cut ½ cup (4 oz/125 g) of the butter into small pieces, add to the pecan-sugar mixture, and, using your fingertips, blend in until the mixture is crumbly. Set aside.

❈ In a large bowl, using an electric mixer, cream together the remaining ½ cup (4 oz/125 g) butter and the remaining ¾ cup (6 oz/190 g) granulated sugar until light and fluffy. Beat in the egg. In another bowl, combine the remaining 2 cups (10 oz/315 g) flour, the baking powder, and the ½ teaspoon ginger. Add to the butter-sugar mixture alternately with the milk.

❈ Spoon the batter into the pan. Sprinkle the berries and nectarine evenly over the batter. Sprinkle the pecan-sugar mixture over the fruit. Bake until the top is golden brown and bubbling and a wooden skewer inserted into the center comes out clean, 45–55 minutes. Let cool in the pan. Cut into squares and place in a transportable container. Serve at room temperature.

serves six to eight | per serving: calories 727 (kilojoules 3,053), protein 8 g, carbohydrates 100 g, total fat 34 g, saturated fat 18 g, cholesterol 105 mg, sodium 168 mg, dietary fiber 4 g

oatmeal chocolate-chunk cookies

These crisp gems are sure to be a hit at any picnic. Accompany with Mocha Brownies (page 106) for a real treat.

- *1¾ cups (9 oz/280 g) all-purpose (plain) flour*
- *½ cup (1½ oz/45 g) rolled oats*
- *1 teaspoon baking soda (bicarbonate of soda)*
- *1 teaspoon salt*
- *1 cup (8 oz/250 g) unsalted butter, at room temperature*
- *1 cup (7 oz/220 g) firmly packed dark brown sugar*
- *½ cup (4 oz/125 g) granulated sugar*
- *1 teaspoon vanilla extract (essence)*
- *2 eggs*
- *2 cups (10 oz/315 g) semisweet (plain) chocolate chunks*
- *¾ cup (3 oz/90 g) chopped walnuts or pecans*

Preheat an oven to 375°F (190°C).

In a small bowl, combine the flour, oats, baking soda, and salt. In a large bowl, using an electric mixer, cream together the butter, sugars, and vanilla. Add the eggs, one at a time, beating well after each addition. Add the flour-oat mixture, a little at a time, and beat until incorporated. Stir in the chocolate chunks and nuts.

Using a tablespoon, drop the batter onto 2 ungreased baking sheets, spacing the cookies about 2 inches (5 cm) apart.

Bake until golden brown, 10–13 minutes. Remove from the oven and let cool on the baking sheets for 2 minutes. Transfer to racks to cool completely. Place in a transportable container or store for up to 1 week in an airtight container.

makes five dozen cookies | per cookie: calories 99 (kilojoules 416), protein 1 g, carbohydrates 12 g, total fat 6 g, saturated fat 3 g, cholesterol 15 mg, sodium 62 mg, dietary fiber 0 g

walnut-orange cake

Brimming with fresh orange zest and juice and ground walnuts, this cake has a crisp exterior and a moist and coarse-textured interior. Serve on its own or with a spoonful of Strawberries with Oranges and Balsamic Vinegar (page 98). It's also good with slices of fresh orange.

1½ cups (6 oz/185 g) chopped
  walnuts

1 cup (5 oz/155 g) all-purpose
  (plain) flour

1 tablespoon baking powder

4 eggs

1½ cups (12 oz/375 g) granulated
  sugar

grated zest and juice of 1 orange
  (about ½ cup/4 fl oz/125 ml juice)

½ cup (4 fl oz/125 ml) extra-virgin
  olive oil

confectioners' (icing) sugar
  for dusting

❋ Preheat an oven to 350°F (180°C). Lightly coat a 9-inch (23-cm) springform pan with olive oil.

❋ Process the walnuts in a food processor until finely ground, almost to the consistency of bread crumbs. In a bowl, combine the ground walnuts, flour, and baking powder.

❋ Place the eggs in a large bowl and beat with an electric mixer until frothy. Slowly add the granulated sugar and beat until the mixture is light, thick, and lemon colored. Slowly add the walnut-flour mixture, beating continuously. Then, with the mixer on low speed, add the orange zest and juice and the olive oil and mix until just combined.

❋ Pour into the prepared pan and bake until a wooden skewer inserted into the center comes out clean, 50–60 minutes. Set the pan on a rack to cool.

❋ Remove the pan sides and transfer the cake to a transportable serving platter. Dust the top with confectioners' sugar, creating a decorative pattern if desired. Serve at room temperature, cut into wedges.

serves eight | per serving: calories 541 (kilojoules 2,272), protein 8 g, carbohydrates 64 g, total fat 30 g, saturated fat 4 g, cholesterol 106 mg, sodium 217 mg, dietary fiber 2 g

strawberries with oranges and balsamic vinegar

A splash of thickened balsamic vinegar enhances this colorful fruit concoction (photo page 97). Serve with your favorite biscotti or with slices of Walnut-Orange Cake (page 96) for a satisfying dessert.

½ cup (4 fl oz/125 ml) balsamic vinegar

4 small blood oranges or other small oranges

3 pt (1½ lb/750 g) strawberries, hulled and halved

✤ Pour the balsamic vinegar into a small saucepan. Place over medium-high heat and boil gently until the vinegar turns syrupy, about 5 minutes. Remove from the heat and let cool.

✤ Using a small, sharp knife, cut a slice off the top and bottom of each orange to expose the fruit. Place each orange upright on a cutting board and slice off the peel in thick strips, cutting around the contour of the orange to expose the flesh. Holding the orange over a transportable bowl, cut along either side of each section, letting the sections drop into the bowl. Remove any seeds and discard.

✤ Add the strawberry halves to the orange sections and stir to combine. Pour the syrup over the fruit and refrigerate for at least 1 hour or for up to 4 hours. Keep chilled until ready to serve.

serves six | per serving: calories 81 (kilojoules 340), protein 1 g, carbohydrates 19 g, total fat 0 g, saturated fat 0 g, cholesterol 0 mg, sodium 2 mg, dietary fiber 5 g

lemon-raspberry squares

These luscious squares (photo at left) have a raspberry jam layer tucked between a crisp sugar-cookie crust and a lemon topping. Make sure to provide forks, paper plates, and plenty of napkins for serving these old-fashioned favorites.

1¾ cups (9 oz/280 g) plus ⅓ cup (2 oz/60 g) all-purpose (plain) flour

½ cup (2 oz/60 g) confectioners' (icing) sugar, plus confectioners' sugar for dusting

½ teaspoon salt

1 cup (8 oz/250 g) chilled unsalted butter, cut into small pieces

1 teaspoon ice water, if needed

1 cup (10 oz/315 g) good-quality raspberry jam

2 cups (1 lb/500 g) granulated sugar

2 teaspoons grated lemon zest

4 eggs, beaten

¾ cup (6 fl oz/180 ml) lemon juice

✻ Preheat an oven to 350°F (180°C). Butter a 9-by-13-inch (23-by-33-cm) baking pan. Place the 1¾ cup (9 oz/280 g) flour, ½ cup (2 oz/60 g) confectioners' sugar, and salt in a food processor and pulse to blend. Add the butter and process until the dough begins to form a ball, adding the ice water if necessary.

✻ Press the dough evenly over the bottom of the prepared baking pan. Bake until the crust is lightly golden, about 20 minutes. Let cool for at least 30 minutes, then evenly spread the jam over the crust.

✻ In a bowl, whisk together the granulated sugar, remaining ⅓ cup (2 oz/ 60 g) flour, and the lemon zest. Place the eggs in a large bowl and slowly add the flour mixture, beating with an electric mixer until well blended, 1–2 minutes. Add the lemon juice and mix to combine.

✻ Pour the lemon mixture carefully over the raspberry jam layer, making sure to keep layers separate. Bake until the lemon topping is just set, 25–30 minutes. Let cool in the pan. Dust with confectioners' sugar and cut into squares with a serrated knife. Place in a transportable container and keep cool until ready to serve.

makes two dozen squares | per square: calories 243 (kilojoules 1,021), protein 3 g, carbohydrates 40 g, total fat 9 g, saturated fat 5 g, cholesterol 57 mg, sodium 64 mg, dietary fiber 0 g

plum-almond tart

Serve this French-style tart with crème fraîche or whipped cream.

for the pastry:

1¼ cups (6½ oz/200 g) all-purpose (plain) flour

1 tablespoon confectioners' (icing) sugar

pinch of salt

½ cup (4 oz/125 g) frozen unsalted butter, cut into small pieces

1 egg yolk

2 tablespoons ice water

for the filling:

1½ cups (6 oz/185 g) sliced (flaked), blanched almonds

¾ cup (6 oz/185 g) plus 2 tablespoons granulated sugar

¼ cup (2 oz/60 g) plus 2 tablespoons unsalted butter, cut into small pieces

2 tablespoons all-purpose (plain) flour

¼ cup (2 fl oz/60 ml) almond liqueur

2 eggs

1¼ lb (625 g) purple plums, pitted and thinly sliced

✳ To make the dough, place the flour, sugar, and salt in a food processor and pulse to blend. Add the butter and process until the mixture resembles coarse meal, 5–10 seconds. With the motor running, add the egg yolk and then the ice water, processing until the dough just begins to form a ball. On a lightly floured work surface, press into a disk. Roll out to fit a 10-inch (25-cm) tart pan with a removable bottom. Transfer the dough to the pan. Trim even with the pan rim and press with your fingers so it adheres to the sides of the pan. Place on a baking sheet and chill while preparing the filling.

✳ Preheat an oven to 400°F (200°C). To make the filling, process the almonds in the food processor until finely ground. Add the ¾ cup (6 oz/ 185 g) sugar, ¼ cup (2 oz/60 g) butter, the flour, and liqueur. Pulse until a paste forms. Add the eggs and process to incorporate. Spread in the dough-lined pan. Top with the plum slices, overlapping them in concentric circles and fitting them tightly together. Fill in the center with 2 rows of plum slices. Dot the plums with the remaining 2 tablespoons butter and sprinkle with the remaining 2 tablespoons sugar. Bake until the top is brown, about 60 minutes. Set on a rack to cool. Remove the pan sides and wrap the tart in aluminum foil to transport. Serve at room temperature, cut into wedges.

serves eight to ten | per serving: calories 495 (kilojoules 2,079), protein 9 g, carbohydrates 51 g, total fat 30 g, saturated fat 13 g, cholesterol 119 mg, sodium 34 mg, dietary fiber 4 g

mixed berry bundt cake

This moist bundt cake is an easy dessert to prepare for a tailgate party. It's also terrific served at an early morning picnic with a big thermos of piping hot coffee. Be sure to select berries that are not overripe or they won't hold up well when baked.

5 eggs

1⅔ cups (13 oz/410 g) sugar

1¼ cups (10 oz/315 g) unsalted butter, at room temperature, cut into small pieces

2 tablespoons kirsch or other fruit liqueur

2½ cups (12½ oz/390 g) all-purpose (plain) flour

1 teaspoon baking powder

pinch of salt

1½ cups (6 oz/185 g) raspberries

1½ cups (6 oz/185 g) blueberries or blackberries

confectioners' (icing) sugar for dusting

❈ Preheat an oven to 325°F (165°C). Butter and flour a 9-inch (23-cm) bundt pan. In a large bowl, blend the eggs and sugar using an electric mixer. Add the butter and liqueur and beat until fluffy. Add all but 2 tablespoons of the flour and the baking powder and salt and beat until well incorporated and no lumps remain.

❈ In another bowl, combine the berries and the reserved 2 tablespoons flour. Toss to coat the berries evenly with the flour. Gently fold the berries into the batter.

❈ Pour the batter into the prepared pan. Bake until a wooden skewer inserted in the center comes out clean, about 60 minutes. Remove from the oven and let cool in the pan for 20–25 minutes. Unmold the cake onto a rack to cool completely.

❈ Dust the top of the cake with confectioners' sugar. Transfer whole to a transportable cake dish or cut into pieces and arrange in a transportable container. Serve at room temperature.

serves ten to twelve | per serving: calories 494 (kilojoules 2,075), protein 7 g, carbohydrates 64 g, total fat 24 g, saturated fat 14 g, cholesterol 154 mg, sodium 90 mg, dietary fiber 2 g

hazelnut cookies

Packaged hazelnuts are available already peeled and sliced.
Toasting develops their full flavor. Serve these buttery nut cookies with
Tropical Fruit Salad with Toasted Coconut (page 55) or
Strawberries with Oranges and Balsamic Vinegar (page 98).

¾ cup (4½ oz/140 g) sliced hazelnuts
(filberts)

½ cup (4 oz/125 g) unsalted butter,
at room temperature

½ cup (3½ oz/105 g) dark brown
sugar

1 teaspoon vanilla extract (essence)

1 egg

¾ cup (4 oz/125 g) all-purpose
(plain) flour

confectioners' (icing) sugar
for dusting (optional)

※ Preheat an oven to 350°F (180°C). Spread the hazelnuts on a baking sheet
and toast until light brown, 3–5 minutes. Remove from the oven and let cool.
Raise the oven temperature to 375°F (190°C).

※ In a bowl, combine the butter and brown sugar and beat with an electric
mixer until well blended. Add the vanilla and egg and continue to beat until
combined. Slowly add the flour, beating until incorporated. Carefully stir in
the toasted hazelnuts.

※ Using a teaspoon, drop the batter onto 2 ungreased baking sheets, spacing
the cookies about 1 inch (2.5 cm) apart. Bake until light brown, about 8 minutes. Transfer the cookies to a rack to cool.

※ Dust the cookies with confectioners' sugar, if desired. Place in a transportable container or store in an airtight container for up to 1 week.

makes about twenty-five cookies | per cookie: calories 100 (kilojoules 420), protein 1 g,
carbohydrates 8 g, total fat 7 g, saturated fat 3 g, cholesterol 18 mg, sodium 5 mg, dietary fiber 1 g

mocha brownies

Instant espresso gives these moist brownies (photo page 94) a delicious mocha flavor. They can be made a day ahead and stored in an airtight container—they will still taste just-baked.

¾ cup (6 oz/180 g) unsalted butter,
  cut into pieces

4 oz (125 g) unsweetened chocolate,
  broken into pieces

2 tablespoons instant espresso powder

1 tablespoon boiling water

2 cups (1 lb/500 g) granulated sugar

4 eggs

1 teaspoon vanilla extract (essence)

1 cup (5 oz/155 g) all-purpose
  (plain) flour

½ teaspoon baking powder

½ teaspoon salt

confectioners' (icing) sugar
  for dusting

✻ Preheat an oven to 350°F (180°C). Butter a 9-by-13-inch (23-by-33-cm) baking pan. In a bowl set over but not touching barely simmering water in a pan, combine the butter and chocolate and stir with a wooden spoon until melted. Let cool.

✻ In a small bowl, dissolve the espresso in the boiling water. Add to the cooled chocolate, then add the granulated sugar, eggs, and vanilla and stir to mix well. In another small bowl, combine the flour, baking powder, and salt. Fold into the chocolate mixture until just incorporated. Pour the batter into the prepared pan. Bake until a wooden skewer inserted into the center comes out slightly fudgy, 25–30 minutes. Set the pan on a rack to cool. Cut 2-inch (5-cm) square brownies. Dust with the confectioners' sugar and place in a transportable container. Serve at room temperature.

makes two dozen brownies | per brownie: calories 186 (kilojoules 781), protein 2 g, carbohydrates 25 g, total fat 9 g, saturated fat 5 g, cholesterol 51 mg, sodium 68 mg, dietary fiber 1 g

index

acknowledgments

The publishers would like to thank Sharilyn Hovind, Ken DellaPenta, Lisa Lee, and Jennifer Hanson for their generous
assistance in producing this book. The photography team wishes to thank Sandra Griswold and Sue Fisher King who kindly lent
props for the photography, as well as Joyce Anna Bowen and the Bonadventura Balloon Company.